GRABBING THE OYSTER!

ANECDOTES & ADVICE
FROM ICONS OF IRISH BUSINESS

Pearce Flannery

OAK · TREE · PRESS

Published by
OAK TREE PRESS
19 Rutland Street, Cork, Ireland
www.oaktreepress.com

© 2008 Pearce Flannery

A catalogue record of this book is
available from the British Library.

ISBN 978 1 904887 25 6

Illustrations by Ken Lee.

Printed in Ireland by ColourBooks.

**All profits from the sale of this book
will go to**

ISPCC

This project is supported by

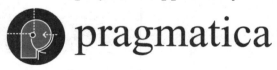

Dedicated to the memory of

Ciara Keenan

CONTENTS

ABOUT THE AUTHOR

Pearce Flannery is the founder and Chief Executive Officer of Pragmatica, the much-acclaimed management, marketing and human resource consultancy group, whose training and motivational programmes are widely recognised as being amongst the most dynamic and innovative in Irish industry today.

Based in Galway, with regional offices in Leixlip and Northampton, Pragmatica's brand is synonymous with the international automotive sector, although it recently opened a division to provide its services to the general commercial sector.

In addition to his position with Pragmatica, Pearce is also a member of the board of the Autopolis Group, widely regarded as the world's leading automotive consultancy group, with offices spanning the globe. He was recently elected to the prestigious position of Fellow of the Institute of the Motor Industry of the United Kingdom.

Pearce's formal qualifications include a BA degree in Economics & Political Science, diplomas in Financial Accounting and in Marketing Practice, and a Master's degree in Business Administration. Pearce won the Marketing Institute's *Marketing Person of the Year* award for 2005 for his work with Pragmatica. He is also a former winner of the JCI / PricewaterhouseCoopers' *Young Entrepreneur of the Year 2006* award.

As the face of Pragmatica, Pearce is widely regarded as the voice of the motor industry and as a premier authority on matters automotive. He appears regularly on RTÉ as a motor industry representative, providing economic and social analysis on programmes such as *Six One News*, *PrimeTime*, *Questions & Answers* and is the contracted automotive analyst for *The Last Word* on Today FM. He also provides comment on a regular basis for the *Business Programme* and *The Right Hook* on Newstalk FM and appears regularly in the national print media.

An accomplished public speaker, Pearce is in constant demand to speak at public functions, conferences and the after-dinner circuit.

He lives in Galway with his wife and family. According to his colleagues, he believes that golf will get easier and that public figures always tell the truth. Pearce believes in dreams!

ACKNOWLEDGEMENTS

I n getting a project such as this onto the bookshelves, a great many people have given freely of their time. I want to thank the entrepreneurs and business people who freely, openly and most generously gave of their time and wisdom. Their enthusiasm for this project was gratifying. I hope I have conveyed the indefinable quality that they all possess and that made them such interesting subjects.

So, in alphabetical order, a special thanks to Denis Brosnan, Louis Copeland, Denis Desmond, Declan Ganley, Liam Griffin, Anne Heraty, Michael Herbert, Pat McDonagh, Padraig Ó Céidigh, Feargal Quinn, Niall Quinn, and James Sheehan.

Many other people have conspired to make this project a success:

- Thanks to all the team at Pragmatica.
- Special mention for Sarah McGauley, John Ryall, Deirdre Nuttall and Padraic Ó Máille.
- Brian O'Kane at Oak Tree Press, who was able to disguise critical evaluation as constructive opinion and temper it with continued motivation.

Finally, in writing a book like this, one spends a lot of time writing and very little time communicating with those around you. So a big 'Thank You' to my wife Orla, and our children Eoghan and Meadbh, for putting up with the chaos.

PREFACE

I have often wondered about successful Irish business people. I have been curious about their ability to succeed. What is it about them? What makes them tick? How do they see opportunity where everybody else sees little or nothing? What goes on in the heads of such people? Is it because there is little enough going on in my own head that I have the capacity to have such thoughts? Do our successful entrepreneurs and business personalities live in some secret place or do they all receive some special education? Are they all related? Are they somehow special? Are they members of some sort of covert super-club for business successes. Is their success pre-ordained? Is it genetic? If so, can we isolate and examine the entrepreneurial gene? Does their success mean that the rest of society comes from the shallow end of the gene pool, so to speak? Most importantly, can the successful characteristics of entrepreneurs be copied?

In short, do they have some special gift?

I have tried to address these questions between these pages. My aim is to uncover the secret formula that makes these guys so enviably successful by letting them tell their stories and provide their insight and opinion on what lies behind the formula for success. Their successes must be examined in the context of the economic and political environment whence they came. In many cases, their backgrounds make their achievements all the more remarkable.

A number of our interview subjects are household names in fields other than business. They have scaled incredible heights in their other lives; however, they are included in this book for their immense achievements as businesspeople. All of our entrepreneurs are included because they have blazed a trail in their respective industries. They typify success. They also typify all that is good in Irish society. They gave of their time, expertise and opinion willingly and without question or persuasion. Given the demands on their time, such generosity is both a rare commodity and commendable for this reason alone.

The interviews with our subjects have been edited in order to ensure that I could document adequately their background and experiences from the wealth of information provided. The accurate recording of so much material has been no easy task. In the interests of clarity and brevity, I have strived in so far as possible to chronicle their personal stories in their own words. This is followed by a section devoted to identifying what it is that makes our subjects so successful in their respective fields of business. I hope that, when you read the book, you will be able to identify what you need to do to enhance your personal chance of commercial success. It is apparent to me that, although specialist knowledge may be required about a particular product or service, comprehensive knowledge alone will not guarantee success.

Successful entrepreneurs **do** have that something extra. There are certain abilities and skills that are common to all of our entrepreneurs. The good news is that these abilities are not genetic or inherent. With a little discipline and application, they can be developed and learnt relatively easily. Successful businesspeople are continually fine-tuning their expertise in this regard. You can develop your own entrepreneurial skills. Without developing these skills, I believe you are unlikely to succeed in your chosen endeavour.

Our entrepreneurs answered their call to action. It is my fervent hope that, when you have finished this book, you will be inspired by such success stories. Maybe you will dare to join them. Hopefully, you will be convinced that we all need to promote the entrepreneurial spirit and realise that the creation of wealth is essential to the economic wellbeing of our country. Ultimately. the creation of wealth is the creation of jobs.

As a scientific study, this book is of limited value. The observations I have drawn are based solely on my personal interpretation of the entrepreneurial characteristics of our subjects. I have used no formal research tools for objective analysis. I cannot support my observations with anything other than the taped interviews, my notes and the goodwill of 12 of Ireland's most successful, experienced, eloquent and good-humoured business people it has been my great fortune to meet.

As a reality check, some of the country's most successful business personalities have bared their souls between these covers. Perhaps I have failed in my mission to analyse our subjects properly or objectively in a scientific sense. I don't really care.

But I **do** care that I do justice to individuals whom I believe have contributed enormously to Irish society. I **do** care that this book is a commercial success, because so many marginalised, abused and disadvantaged children will benefit if this project is a success. I will welcome criticism, because it will mean that someone somewhere has bought another copy of the book. Will I take criticism on board? Probably not. But I will thank you for contributing to a very worthy cause.

The ISPCC and Childline provide support to the weakest and most marginalised members of our society: our children. The fact that the ISPCC needs to exist, not to mind fundraise, is evidence that our society has not yet evolved and reached its true potential. The very facts that sections of our community need organisations such as this demonstrate that we have a long way to go in our social development.

Organisations such as the ISPCC and Childline protect us from the worst excesses of a society we ourselves have created. We all have a duty of care to our children. We created the problems facing them, so the least we can do is to support the agencies that have the motivation to deal with them. In other words, we must support them in any way we can – in this instance, by purchasing a copy of this book and ensuring that your friends and colleagues do likewise. There is a responsibility on us to ensure that such organisations are not starved of the resources they need to provide such essential services.

In summary, therefore, this book is based only on opinion, assumption and supposition. What you read in these pages is a matter of opinion – my opinion. So, even if you think the content is rubbish, go and buy another copy. Give it to your friends and tell them to buy another copy to give to their friends.

Because, one way or another, we should all care!

Pearce Flannery
September 2008

1
FACING THE CURRENT ECONOMIC REALITY

It is a generally accepted commercial practice that the requirement to make real economic change or to take a calculated business gamble requires that a person commit to two fundamental activities:

- Confronting the reality of the environment in which you currently find yourself.
- Taking some form of real action to change that reality.

In this regard, anyone with a personal or professional interest in business must evaluate the current macro-economic environment that we now face. It is essential that we critically evaluate our economic position, with a view to forecasting what direction our economy may take going forward. We need to try to make future projections based on current information. This is a difficult, and often subjective, task.

This chapter is my attempt to do just that. It may conflict with your personal viewpoint. It may be appear to be contentious and be construed as somewhat of a personal rant. In some ways, it is. The core problems facing both our society and economy are often overlooked, because we are conditioned to evaluate the issues according to accepted indicators, which have been given their measure of importance by a bloated, inefficient and complacent political establishment over many years. This is the way they have always done it and this is the way they will do it now – even if it is patently obvious that it is the wrong direction to take and doomed to fail. This is typical of political inertia. Such political inertia will be a millstone around the neck of Ireland's future prosperity. So if this is perceived to be a personal rant or crusade, then so be it. It does not make my observations or opinion any less correct.

At the time of writing, we are on the downturn of Ireland's most successful and prosperous economic performance since Partition. These are indeed challenging economic times. The problems both domestic and international are accepted generally. Domestically, we have had an over-reliance on the construction sector as the driver of economic prosperity. Internationally, the dual problems of fiscal recklessness by many financial institutions and poor international management on the energy markets have conspired to make our predicament precarious at best.

At this stage, these are familiar and well-documented issues. The symptoms and problems of our economic health have been identified by many eminent social and economic commentators. What is less well documented, however, is the actual root cause of our problems. What – or who – actually allowed the symptoms to go untreated and to develop into the current situation, whereby we all face potentially unprecedented economic hardship. Why do our elected representatives consistently refuse to face current realities until it is too late?

The unfortunate truth of the matter is that they are incapable of pre-empting problems and unwilling to proactively address issues, because such positive action may impinge on their popularity in their local area and, ultimately, cost them votes. This has led us to the regrettable situation whereby political gombeenmen, who place personal ambition and party loyalty ahead of national progress, are in charge of the destiny of this nation.

The problems with the macro-economic environment are symptoms of the reality we now face. The fundamental problem is political ineptitude and continued economic mismanagement. Political ineptitude has been our most limiting economic factor for over 30 years and seems destined to continue for the foreseeable future. Many of our elected representatives have neither the requisite training, experience nor ability to manage an economy.

This can only be addressed through a radical overhaul of our electoral system. An electoral system designed in Britain in the 18th century is patently unsuitable for an ambitious and aggressive economy, aiming to be at the cutting edge of international trade in the 21st century. We need to dispense with the single transferable voting system and curtail the number of sitting TDs in Dáil Éireann; 166

sitting (sometimes) TDs, representing 26 counties, is ridiculous, inefficient and expensive. In addition to this, Seanad Éireann and an extensive network of County and Urban Councillors also support these representatives. Our electoral system has become an ogre and needs to be culled – immediately.

Because of the inability of successive Irish Governments to manage our economy competently, Irish entrepreneurs and business leaders have had to be amongst the most accomplished and capable in the world. These people are the real drivers of our economy.

On the domestic front, Ireland has been the beneficiary of an immense financial windfall from the EU over the last 30 years. We have received hundreds of billions of Euro in aid. This massive financial windfall has papered over the cracks and hidden the fact that our elected representatives have been often incompetent and mediocre at best. This is true across all the political parties, with a few notable individual exceptions.

Paradoxically, this windfall has inadvertently created a monster, in the sense that such economic riches have cultivated an acceptance of political mediocrity. Politicians with little or no ability have been able to hide behind a prosperity that has been primarily driven by Brussels, and not Dublin. Over the years, many of our TDs and, indeed, many of our cabinet members are notable more for their profile than their achievements. In the majority of cases, their only accomplishment was to distribute this financial largesse in such a fashion as to maximise their vote in their local area.

If we subtract the infrastructural and economic progress made directly as a result of EU subvention, the true economic story would be dramatically different. Add in the fact that, over the last number of years, the construction sector has been responsible for a staggering 24% contribution to our nation's GDP and we begin to see the real story and the true extent of the financial mismanagement of this country. This mismanagement is now, and has been, a direct result of gross ineptitude and incompetence in Government.

This is evidenced by the difficulty that successive Taoisigh have had in finding an effective and competent team for many portfolios at cabinet level. The crutch of EU membership has enabled many ineffectual elected representatives to avoid exposure for what they really are. An electoral system built on clientelism and parish-pump politics sustains this situation by ensuring that we do not foster the development of enough competent statesmen. Given the problems in finding only 16 capable individuals for cabinet posts, the lack of quality personnel in the back benches must be at laughable proportions. To put it simply, our electoral system ensures we elect 'pothole-fillers, not statesmen'; these people are utterly incapable of managing an economy.

Likewise many of the current international economic crises have developed through the unfortunate and coincidental emergence of largely incompetent international leaders. It appears to be our bad luck that such a number of them have arrived together. Look at members of the G8, for example: George W Bush, Gordon Browne, Nicolas Sarkozy, and Silvio Berlusconi. All under immense pressure in their respective countries. All appear incapable or unable to cope with the fundamentals of an economic crisis. This is the first time we have seen the simultaneous emergence of such ineffective leaders, all in step with one another. It is a unique occurrence. This is the primary driver of the current international economic crisis and its associated problems. It is no coincidence that such political ineptitude is accompanied by the economic upheaval that we all face today. The current international economic uncertainty is as a result of the election of showmen and celebrity politicians over those with a proven record of achievement.

Nonetheless, over 15 years of unprecedented economic success has resulted in many positive spillovers to the socio-economic fabric of Ireland. There has been much notable progress. It should be acknowledged that we have also had a few high achievers on the political front. Many such achievers were driven out as a direct result of their successes and subsequent popularity. Some of our most competent performers hold EU portfolios, primarily because of domestic political skullduggery. Europe's gain is Ireland's loss. Others just gave up the ghost when faced with such an intransigent establishment. A small few remain fighting against the tide of mediocrity.

It is important to note that the fundamental driver of our economic success over the last 15 years has not been the Irish Government. It happened because of the availability of low interest rates and cheap money on the international money markets. Low interest rates and the availability of cheap money are outside the control of the Irish government. Ireland's prosperity is not a result of our national fiscal policy.

This last decade has seen much overt prosperity. However, if we leave the wealthy and institutionally-funded property development sector aside, the picture is slightly different. The real drivers of an economy's wealth are not the property developers. We can see the evidence of this at the time of writing. Property-driven investment and employment has all but dried up and its contribution to the national exchequer is radically diminished. Property speculation only makes a fleeting contribution to the economic health of any society.

Today, we are erroneously fed the line that we are on the cusp of recession. This is untrue. It is a blatant cover-up. Ireland has been in real-time recession since 2004. It is impossible to believe that the government did not see that the income from stamp duty was entirely disproportionate to the returns from an economy in a healthy state. The acceptable level of influence of the construction sector on a country's GDP is in the region of 10% to 12%; we doubled this, without even a murmur. The banking sector has been complicit in this charade, with such immoral strategies as offering 100% mortgages over 40 years, with only lip service being paid to stress-testing. The government hid the inherent weaknesses in the economy, in a drive to maintain stamp duty income at any cost. This approach necessitated a concerted emphasis on ensuring that property values continued to increase, irrespective of the long-term consequences. Such an economic strategy, by elected representatives with a public service mandate, was both immoral and wrong. When questioned about an overheated construction sector and the imminent property collapse, they invented the wonderful and fictitious term of a 'soft landing'. Where is the much-heralded 'soft landing' now?

Long-term sustainable wealth creation for Ireland can only come from the further development of internationally-traded goods and services. As an open economy, dependent on international trade, we need to position ourselves at the cutting edge in the provision of research and development, value-added or intellectually-driven industry. Many of the entrepreneurs profiled in the following pages have succeeded in doing just that, in a variety of different ways, in many diverse industries.

In my opinion, we must focus our future efforts on moving up the supply chain into areas such as R&D and the development of intellectually-driven niche specialities. We must immediately shift our strategy from a goods for export-oriented, labour-driven society; our long-term future depends on developing a commercially-traded services sector, providing added value from indigenous Irish industry in a knowledge-based economy.

If, as an economy, we succeed in this endeavour, we could be looking at a radically different type of entrepreneur in years to come. Perhaps their intrinsic personal characteristics may be similar but, if the entrepreneur of the future is to emulate the achievements of the success stories within these pages, we must develop an environment that empowers them. We must demand leadership and concerted action from our Government. If we are to drive the strategic change required, we must empower our change agents in areas such as finance, education, entrepreneurship and, especially, in our infrastructure. To drive the change necessary, we must first all face up to the current reality.

The reality is that our infrastructural development is appalling. One only has to look at the rate of our broadband rollout or our abysmal public transport and health systems for evidence of this fact. This situation has highlighted the fact that the long-term socio-economic health of our economy is dependent on people like the entrepreneurs examined in this book. These, and many others like them, are the real drivers of the success of this country.

Only 11% of Irish exports come from Irish-owned companies. Yet over 75% of Irish business is family-owned, a sector that gets little formal State support or acknowledgement. These are worrying statistics, as they highlight the fact that we are not paying sufficient attention to the empowerment of indigenous Irish and family-owned business. In a peripheral open island economy such as ours, this sector will continue to be the economic engine room of our society for many years to come.

The achievements of our interview subjects have been all the more remarkable when one considers the inhospitable environment that has faced the creation of wealth and employment in Ireland over the last few decades. Thankfully, the hostile culture of suspicion, negativity and begrudgery that once faced Irish entrepreneurs is becoming a thing of the past. To put it simply, we do not have a history of fostering corporate and commercial development. Historically, it is not in our psyche. For far too long, the entrepreneurial spirit in Ireland has been branded as 'cute-hoorism' and treated with disdain and distrust. As a nation, we must change our mindset in this regard if we are to continue to prosper. We must dispense with the over-emphasis on regulation, bureaucracy, red tape and other such obstacles to job creation. Such burdens place undue pressures on fledgling businesses and restrict their potential for success.

Achieving success in the business sector has become even more difficult of late, as our competitiveness has been eroded. Especially, as our wage inflation has continued to race ahead of many of our international economic competitors. Benchmarking and ill-advised social partnership agreements have been key drivers in our wage inflation. In addition, our favourable corporation tax rates are being replicated in Eastern Europe and our autonomy in the levying of favourable tax rates will be ceded eventually to Brussels. At the time of writing, the country had just given a resounding "No" to the Lisbon treaty. Only time will tell whether this was an inspired decision or simply the negative reactions of a disgruntled and disillusioned electorate.

Whatever happens, we will need clear and effective economic and political direction going forward. We will be able to rely no longer on the EU to help us out of our problems; most probably, we will be required to manage our economy from indigenously-raised finance. This is a big challenge for people whose current mindset could not deliver the goods in times of plenty. Challenging circumstances always sort the men out from the boys. Perhaps this is one positive to be taken from the current difficult situation.

In the fullness of time, we will come to acknowledge that people like our entrepreneurs will have been the economic saviours of Ireland. Our indigenous entrepreneurs are the people who influence our employment figures, our Gross Domestic Product and, ultimately, the living standards of our citizens. Many builders and developers have created great wealth for themselves and good luck to them, they should enjoy it. After all they did take the risks, and fortune favours the brave.

Our entrepreneurs, on the other hand, have created wealth for both themselves and the country. They have created sustainable wealth. They have contributed handsomely to the society whence they came. We owe people like these a great deal, because it is they who have ensured that the environment that faces our children will be a much more temperate place than the one that faced us growing up in the 1970s or 1980s.

I sincerely hope when you read this book that you will come to the conclusion that we should applaud our entrepreneurs. We should fête them, revere them and, above all, try to emulate them. We should thank them, for these are the type of people who really do make this country what it is. They should be recognised for their contribution to industry and to society at large.

The climate for people establishing new businesses in Ireland has improved immensely over the last decade, although I do not believe that the statutory bodies tasked with such developments have been the primary drivers of this revolution. They have continued to operate as they have always done, with some notable, but isolated, successes. But for the entrepreneur whose plans do not pigeonhole neatly into one of their templates, there is little support. Very often, they are forced to plough their own lonely and difficult furrow.

The key driver for these people has been a ready access to cheap credit and finance. Budding entrepreneurs no longer can assume the availability of cheap funds and credit, however. Given the uncertain international environment in the fields of finance and energy and the domestic constraints facing industrial and commercial development at present, we need to nurture the environment and the entrepreneurial mindset that encourages commercial creativity.

As the paradigm is now shifting, we need to convince our elected representatives and the relevant representative bodies that the State needs to develop a more conducive fiscal environment for start-up businesses. We need more tax breaks for start-up indigenous business, with lower VAT thresholds, corporate taxes and a complete abolition of employer's PRSI for businesses employing people for a minimum of a two-year formative period. This country has been fostering an environment of negativity towards wealth and employment creation for far too long. It will only change if you shout "Stop". This is a call to action, one that will be covered in a later chapter. We all need to answer this call to action.

The following chapters contain the personal stories of 12 of Ireland's leading business personalities, told in their own words. They have heard their call to action. They have answered this call and achieved phenomenal results. They realised that the world could, and would, be their oyster; all they had to do was grab it. So they did.

This is their story.

PART 1

THEY DID IT!

I am monarch of all I purvey.
My value there's none will dispute.
If you come for my provisions today,
Your taste and your pocket I'll suit.

The Cry of the Dublin Market Trader, c.1900

2

DENIS BROSNAN

Denis Brosnan served with the Kerry Group from 1972 until 2002, and is now primarily involved in healthcare. Under his leadership, the Kerry Group grew from a small, regional dairy co-operative to one of the world's leading food suppliers, employing more than 14,000 people around the world.

Brosnan is now a dominant figure in both care provision, particularly in the United Kingdom, and producing and raising thoroughbred horses for the racing industry on his stud farm in Croom, Co. Limerick. He also chairs Horse Racing Ireland, the Irish horseracing authority.

A SCÉIL FHÉIN

I 've been living in Limerick since the 1980s, but I was born just outside Tralee in 1944. To this day, I'm a Kerry supporter. My parents were farmers. They met when my mother, then a teacher, was working in London with my father's sisters. After they married, they settled down to running the farm and bringing up their three children: my older brother, my sister and myself.

I went to National School a mile away from home, and later to St. Brendan's Secondary School which, although it was just 25 miles away, I attended as a boarder. Straight after school, I went to University College Cork, where I studied what was then called Dairy Science (now Food Science), taking my studies to Masters level. My education played a big part in my development in terms of being away from home and learning to stand very much on my own. Between secondary school and university, I spent 10 years away from the family being educated and the lessons I acquired in self-sufficiency and independence were much more important than anything I learned from books.

Nowadays, we assume a generally high standard of education for most people. Completing secondary and third level education is now the norm rather than the exception and, while there will always be some people who enjoy great success without having had much formal education, training is hugely important, both in the direct provision of skills and also in fostering confidence. Now, we see graduates emerging from schools and universities who know that they have what it takes to do well. At the same time, the links between business and higher education have grown substantially, which is good. While this process is moving in the right direction, it would be even better if we could speed it up, as the Irish economy does need a further boost from our home-grown entrepreneurs if it is to continue doing well.

When I graduated in 1967, I worked briefly as a salesman for a Scottish chemical company, selling industrial detergents. One day, I visited Golden Vale as a salesman and met up with Dave O'Loughlin, who told me that I was wasting my time and that he had a better job for me. I spent four and a half years in Golden Vale, including a year in

London, where I was employed as the company's export sales executive.

At the end of 1972, the then chairman of Kerry, Eddie Hayes, asked me to come and work for Kerry in Ireland, which I did. Moving from London was a bit of a wrench at the time, as it's a city that I've always loved very much. At that time, Kerry Co-op was still just a vision. Eddie was a very well-known chairman, and a member of the co-ordinating body for co-operatives. He was a man with great vision, and a big influence on me in the early years of my career.

My education played a big part in my development
in terms of being away from home and
learning to stand very much on my own.

I n those days, the Irish dairy industry was in a state of transition. A lot of things were happening in the country generally. In 1973, Ireland joined what was then called the EEC, and everything started to change, not least in agriculture and industry. The many little creameries dotted around the country started merging into a smaller number of larger organisations, the big co-operatives. This was a good move for farmers, and gave them new insights into how to make money from their product. In the late 1960s and early 1970s, five dairy co-operatives dominated the Irish market, including Golden Vale and Mitchelstown; they were known as the 'Big Five'. As County Kerry was producing 15% of the country's milk, and selling much of it to external creameries, Eddie's vision at the time was for Kerry to become a major player.

One of the challenges that we had to battle with constantly during the early years was an issue that companies still face today: getting the right financing to get things done. The problem was always that, when we didn't have a lot of money, it was hard to get a loan. This catch-22 is hard to navigate. Without money, it's very difficult to build a name and reputation and, without a name and reputation, it is very difficult to get financing. This is just as difficult now as it was then, and it remains a serious challenge to Irish entrepreneurs today, and one that we will have to look closely at as a nation if we really want to encourage successful business.

In my early days at Kerry, the environment in Ireland was certainly one in which the government and everybody else tried to be helpful, but the problem was that the country was very far from being prosperous. The Industrial Development Authority, now known as Enterprise Ireland, was enormously helpful in terms of encouraging investment in the food industry and in other sectors, and it's important to recognise the useful role played by government policy in these years, and the IDA's contribution to the modern Ireland. However, the emphasis in those days was on encouraging foreign businesses to come to Ireland, to create jobs and to help the Irish workers to stay at home. The consciousness that the Irish could compete on the world stage had not yet become part of the culture.

One can hear people saying that customers have become more demanding over the years, but I believe that the fundamentals of business have remained the same over the years. People expect a good service and all that goes with it, and the greater the demand for a product or service, the better it will be. In my experience, it is just as easy to provide a wonderful service as a sloppy service, regardless of the scale of the enterprise. It's crucial to develop and foster a culture of being the best, from start to finish. In the early days, I learned a hugely important lesson from Jim Donovan, the Sales Director at Golden Vale, which was that it was not our job to be slick salesmen, but people who said, "We will do things better" – and then followed it through. Quite simply, doing things better was good business practice then, and it is still good business practice now. Throughout the 1970s, we used this approach initially to transform Kerry into one of the 'Big Six' in the Irish dairy business, and then to move beyond that. By the 1990s, people from all over the world were coming to see how Kerry operated, so that they could use our techniques and business practices in their own organisations.

Irish people always had the potential to excel
as entrepreneurs and business people;
it just took them a while to realise it.

When I started with Kerry, the Irish way of doing business was different to that in the USA or the UK, but that's not the case any more. Now, all the same norms apply, from business ethics to business standards. Ireland's business culture has changed a great deal. The reasons why are manifold, but one thing that is clear is that the Irish people *always* had the potential to excel as entrepreneurs and business people; it just took them a while to realise it. Many of the Irish who went to the USA, the UK and further afield were hugely successful but, until comparatively recently, the ones who stayed at home just didn't seem to have the confidence to achieve all they could. I'm not sure why; perhaps it was something to do with the way that they were educated. Confidence is key to success. While the IDA did a lot of fantastic work during this period, it took far too long to recognise what Irish entrepreneurs could contribute. The idea that the only way that Ireland could be prosperous was to invite foreign investment and foreign companies made Ireland second class from the outset, with the general impression being that the Irish couldn't do things all that well, and foreigners had to be brought in to teach us. Gradually, this changed, as Irish people began to succeed, first in their own country, and then all over the world. I worked through the period in which Ireland's consciousness about itself changed. The Irish themselves had always been capable of greatness. What changed was that they began to realise it.

Joining the European Union had a lot to do with the changes in Irish business culture, and so did a general shift in attitude towards the much more confident, self-assured climate that we have today. Increasing levels of education certainly played a major part, not just in the transmission of skills, as going through third level education became the norm, but also in helping young Irish people develop confidence in their own innate skills and abilities. Seeing Irish businesses succeed also played an important role in growing Irish people's awareness of all the great things that they can achieve. As it grew, the Kerry Group contributed a lot to the Irish economy and, more importantly, it also contributed a sense of competence and awareness of aptitude to a new generation of Irish people who could look to the example of everyone who was doing well within the Kerry organisation, and think, "I could do that too!". Similarly, within the organisation, we grew more assured of our own capabilities.

Anyone who really wants to succeed must have vision
but, even more importantly, they must have
absolute commitment, and be prepared to put in
all the hours of the day, days of the week and weeks of the
year that it takes to succeed. Anyone who can do this, while
remaining absolutely focussed, will invariably succeed.

One day, in about 1980, a group of us sat down and decided that it was time for Kerry to move beyond Ireland. We initially opened an office in London and one in Chicago. By now, we were also confident that we had access to capital, which had been a limiting factor in the earlier days. Most importantly, however, was that we had learned to be unapologetic about our strengths and capabilities. We had realised that we were actually a lot better than many of our foreign competitors, and more than able to operate in their patch as well as our own. From this point on, we never looked back. Our approach translated very well to our enterprises in other countries, too. Whether in Brazil, Mexico, America, or wherever, our message to the employees was that we expected a certain standard from Kerry people; we expected them to be winners. Whatever the culture, everybody wants to be part of a winning team, and our people around the world learned how to perform at a standard that they had never thought possible. They just had to learn, as the Irish had, that they were all capable of winning.

In business, as elsewhere, one finds many different types of people. Some entrepreneurs relish team work, and others find it hard to work with others and can be hugely successful only when they can keep things small and do things by themselves. Others can only succeed when they can spread their vision, commitment and passion amongst a great number of people. At Kerry, we succeeded very much in having an overall organisational culture rather than individual entrepreneurs. Our employees learned that they were Kerry first and Mexican, or Brazilian or American second.

It's crucial to develop and foster a culture of being the best,
from start to finish.

Of course, we made some mistakes along the way. The person or business that never makes mistakes doesn't get very far! The secret is to make fewer mistakes than any of one's competitors. To speak for myself and Kerry, the biggest errors we made were the companies we didn't buy than any of the ones we did. The biggest mistake I ever made was during a period when we were supplying cheese to the pizza industry in the USA during the mid-1980s. The company was run by some good friends of mine and, when they showed me around, they advised me to start up a big pizza factory in Ireland, predicting that all the Europeans would be eating pizza soon. "That stuff will never catch on!" was my response.

In 1986, Kerry ceased trading as a co-operative and became a PLC. In 1988, we bought an American company that was actually bigger than Kerry at the time, because we knew that we could run it better. This was the start of a whole new era for Kerry. Over the course of the next 16 years, we expanded our business to many countries around the world, including the USA, Canada, Mexico, Brazil, Argentina, Southeast Asia, Malaysia, China and on to Australia and New Zealand. At that time, only a minuscule number of Irish companies could be found in most of these countries, but now Irish companies are operating in every corner of the globe. At the time of Kerry's great expansion, I spent a huge amount of my time travelling. In fact, the reason why we settled in Limerick was to be close to Shannon Airport. Travelling was just something I had to do, but I certainly would not relish the prospect of living that way again. Living from a suitcase is exhausting. While I was making my way around the world, my wife Joan was at home with our small children, and I often used to tell her that she had the easy job! It was stressful being in Sao Paolo or Singapore and knowing that I'd have to spend another weekend away from home because there was more work to be done the following week, all the while wishing I was with my family. I was away for half of every month, flying from Shannon to London and from there to Singapore, China, New Zealand … I wouldn't wish it on anyone!

Fortunately, modern technology – the Internet, mobile phones, and so on – has reduced the extent to which business people have to travel somewhat. Today, I still need to travel, but now it's usually a case of just a night or two away from home.

I believe that there would be many more successful companies in Ireland today, if only there was better and easier access to funding.

I n 1991, while still very much involved with Kerry, I became Chairman of the Irish Horseracing Authority, Horse Racing Ireland, and got involved in modernising the Irish thoroughbred industry, which is one of the biggest and probably the most successful in the world. For thoroughbred horses born each year, we are only surpassed by the USA and Australia. For a small island, that's not bad! Fifteen thousand people are directly employed, so it is a very significant industry here. At the time of my appointment, the Irish government was led by Charles Haughey, and successive governments over the course of the next 17 years continued to use my services in the industry. I have always had an enormous passion for horses; that's why we run a stud farm at Croom House in Co. Limerick today.

The thoroughbred industry is immensely difficult and complex, with many players, which means that any modernisation or transformation occurs only as quickly as the slowest-moving part. Each sector feels that it's the most important, from the people who own or breed horses through to trainers, riders, bookmakers, racecourses, or the governing body for integrity. Making things even more complicated is the fact that the industry is also controlled by international committees that ensure, for example, that major races don't compete with each other. The racing industry also is driven very much by market forces. Throughout the long era when farmers operated within a quota system, with quotas for milk, beef and so forth, the horseracing industry was out there in the world market place competing for sales or races to be won.

The Irish thoroughbred industry is one of the biggest,
and probably the most successful, in the world.

B y 2002, I had spent 35 years in the food industry and, at 57, felt
I had had enough of travelling frantically around the world, so
I thought that I would retire and concentrate on raising horses
on our stud farm in Croom, Co. Limerick. However, I found myself,
together with a small group of investors, getting heavily into a new
business in the care industry after a foray into the leisure industry.
Initially, we put together a fund to invest in nursing homes, but now
the care industry is a huge interest for us, and we are running nursing
homes, psychiatric homes, schools and crèches in the United Kingdom
and, more recently, the United States and Ireland. The care industry is
a huge sector, because there is a burning need everywhere for people
to care for those who need it, from babies to older people. We believe
that any system that looks after people well and ensures that nothing
detracts from their dignity is going to do well. Our group is now
known in the UK as the biggest company in care; my attempt to retire
was not exactly a resounding success! I often say that I would like to
achieve in the care industry in 10 years what we did in Kerry in 30. We
started out in 2002, so perhaps by 2012 that dream will have been
achieved, and I can really retire.

I find many Irish entrepreneurs wholly admirable in their way of
doing things; I'd hesitate to isolate just one or two. My generation is
now at the stage of beginning to think about retirement, and a whole
new generation of younger people is emerging. The basic factors for
success have not changed in the interim. First of all, anyone who really
wants to succeed must have vision, but even more importantly they
must have absolute commitment, and be prepared to put in all the
hours of the day, days of the week and weeks of the year that it takes
to succeed. Anyone who can do this, while remaining absolutely
focussed, will invariably succeed. The saying "It's not over until the fat
lady sings" is true in business. Successful entrepreneurs are like
winning sports people. They are focussed. They have rationalised and
understood the opposition. They will follow the game through right to
the very end, staying tough and absolutely focussed all the way,

because no sale is complete until the money has been handed over and no game is won until the final whistle. Without that absolute commitment and focus, you might get lucky three times out of five but it won't happen every time, and you won't emerge as the overall winner. A man for whom I have great admiration is Padraig Harrington, who is a person who has the vision to succeed, and who follows that vision through with total focus and commitment every single step of the way.

Fortunately, in Ireland, we have superseded most of the significant barriers to successful entrepreneurship, above all in achieving the levels of confidence that we now enjoy, so those who do demonstrate serious passion and commitment can achieve their aims. I have mentioned the difficulties that the Kerry Group had in securing the financing that it needed in the early days, and unfortunately this is a problem that new companies continue to face today. In fact, I believe that there would be many more successful companies in Ireland today, if only there was better and easier access to funding. New companies can turn to state agencies, and they can turn to banks. But finding complete, reliable funding can still be difficult. Over the past three decades, we have shown that Irish entrepreneurs can even make a greater contribution than inward investment and so we must continue and extend our support of them. State agencies have already made huge contributions in this area, and there is so much more than they can do, especially because they are in a position to take on greater risk than the banks. While two out of five new enterprises will collapse, three will succeed and they will be of enormous benefit to the economy.

Successful entrepreneurs are like winning sports people.
They are focussed. They have rationalised and understood
the opposition. They will follow the game through right to
the very end, staying tough and absolutely focussed all the
way, because no sale is complete until the money has been
handed over and no game is won until the final whistle.

I reland has shown it can be a number one player on the world stage, with industries such as CRH or Kerry, with entertainers such as U2 or sportsmen such as Padraig Harrington or Aidan O'Brien. What is wonderful, for today's younger entrepreneurs, is that they no longer have to battle with the presupposition that Irish people cannot go global and succeed. In recent years, Ireland has attracted a lot of young people from other countries, particularly from Eastern Europe. Many of these cultures have a lot in common with Ireland; once proud nations that endured many years of colonisation. I think that we will also see great things from these people, whether they stay in Ireland or go home. Currently, their economies are decades behind us, but I believe that they will catch up very quickly.

The first time I retired, I went into the care industry and even if I'm not working quite as hard as I was before, I'm still working. Maybe in five to 10 years I'll really retire, and the next time I do, I will definitely, absolutely retire.

Ireland has shown it can be a number one player on the world stage, with industries such as CRH or Kerry, with entertainers such as U2, or sportsmen such as Padraig Harrington or Aidan O'Brien.

3
LOUIS COPELAND

Louis Copeland is Ireland's best-known tailor and menswear retailer. The Copeland family have been in the clothing business for nearly 100 years in Ireland. Hyman Copeland started the business in the early 1900s, which was continued by his son, Louis. Today, the business is run by the third generation, namely Louis and Adrian.

Louis Copeland is the eponymous owner / manager of Louis Copeland Men's Clothing, Ireland's most prestigious gentleman's outfitters, with branches in Dublin and Galway. The store won the *FBD Crest Retail Excellence* award in 2007, in recognition of its consistently high standards. The business was founded by his father more than eight decades ago, and continues to grow under the current owner's supervision. A younger generation of Copelands is now entering the business, which is poised to complete its first century in grand style.

A SCÉIL FHÉIN

The Copelands first entered the Irish scene when my grandfather came from Russia and settled here. Originally Jewish, he married an Irish girl, converted to Catholicism and set up business as a tailor in the city; that means that Copeland's have been supplying Irish men with suits since 1908! Possibly, my grandfather's family was in the tailoring business for years prior to that date too, I just don't know.

My grandfather was Louis, my father was Louis, I'm Louis and my son, and now grandson, also have the family name, so we are taking care of future generations! In any case, it was my father who started the current business, Louis Copeland, about 80 years ago. He started off in business as a tailor and a cutter, working out of rooms on Capel Street. He also worked in various other places. In fact, he worked with Ben Dunne senior in Roches Stores in Dublin, and also in Cork, when Dunne opened a shop down there, so my father and Ben Dunne knew each other rather well.

I grew up in Drumcondra in Dublin, just around the corner from the former Taoiseach, Bertie Ahern. Bertie and I grew up together. Until the age of 14, I attended St. Patrick's School in Drumcondra, but I was introduced to the business at eight or 10. Even at that early age, I would take the bus into Capel Street, and I would be given messages to run, and tasks like sweeping the floor and so forth.

After leaving St. Patrick's at 14, I attended a technical school on Parnell Square for about three years, studying textiles. After that, before going into my father's business officially, I worked in a factory in an old place up on High Street called the Two Owls, John Barron & Company. Two years later, I went into the business on Capel Street, where I am still based today.

Working with my father so closely and from an early age means that I can clearly identify him as my primary educator in business, and I suppose I could refer to him as a mentor.

I did not go to university and, in some ways, I regret this today; there's a little voice in the back of my head that suggests sometimes that maybe I should have had more education. It does not worry me, and things worked out well for me anyway but I do think that nowadays a good education is very important, and a university background very necessary for the younger generation. That is not to say that it is impossible to do well without a university education, because people with natural talent and ability will always do well, but I feel strongly that a good education is an excellent background now, in providing an outline of knowledge and understanding.

Of course, education should go hand-in-hand with the right attitude for business, and that's not really something that can be learned. Those who have it will do well in business, and those who don't will fall out of the system and go into something else. With a good foundation in education and the right attitude, the best way to learn is to get on the floor and start interacting with people and with experienced staff. Working in a clothing shop like ours is one of the best experiences that can be gained. Someone who has worked well in a clothing shop can work anywhere, because they are used to dealing with, and interacting with, people.

It is hugely important that staff members are happy in their work, because when they are not, customers can sense it, and it has a negative impact on their experience of the business.

S tarting from my very early role in the business as a little boy, you could say I evolved into the role I fill today.

Over the years, Louis Copeland, the business, has changed a lot. There was a time when it provided only made-to-measure suits, which were made in our workshop. In those days, we had just one shop and about 30 people working on suits. We sold no accessories at all. Nowadays, about 90% of our business is off-the-peg, and we don't just sell suits anymore; increasingly, we carry a lot of casual wear, as well as all the accessories.

A successful business has to change with the times, or it won't survive, and Irish culture has changed a lot over the years. With respect to dress, things are completely different. As recently as 20 years ago, a typical man had just one suit and possibly two shirts and a couple of ties, usually a dark navy one and perhaps a wine one as well;

that was it! Nowadays, men have wardrobes full of suits and accessories to match. It's all very different. At the same time, the business of selling clothes is immeasurably different. Thirty years ago, Louis Copeland was a 'corner shop'. It had its niche. Nowadays, business is global, and people travel a lot. That means that we are in competition with everybody! Our customers can travel and buy clothes abroad, and shops from overseas can come over here and set up businesses.

We have a number of core markets. The people who are buying suits for occasions represent one. Just look at the number of people getting married – and I thought that marriage was going out of fashion! Before, wedding parties would rent dress suits or morning suits, but now the thing seems to be to invest in a nice suit. We see a lot of grooms coming in with their fathers and best men to buy a suit. Of course, we also sell a lot to businessmen, as suits are essentially their uniform. This is changing a little bit, insofar as more men are wearing smart casual clothes to work as an alternative to a suit, which is one of the reasons why we have expanded our range. We opened a shop in the IFSC in Dublin recently, and I was impressed by the number of men who were not wearing suits to work.

Our premises on Capel Street is just around the corner from the Four Courts, and we do a lot of business with the barristers, lawyers and solicitors who work there, as well as supplying the frock coats, waistcoats and the gowns for the judiciary. We also do rather a lot of costume-making for films made in Ireland, both by Irish and by foreign film-makers, mostly outfits for contemporary films rather than period costumes. We also get some unusual requests; we made Dustin the Turkey's outfit for the 2008 *Eurovision Song Contest*! He wore a white Elvis-style jumpsuit with a cape.

A couple of times every year, we have a man coming in to buy a suit for his father. He'll give us the size and choose a colour, but when we ask whether his father can come in for a fitting, the answer is "No, we'll turn up the trousers ourselves" – the reason is that the gentleman is deceased! For a lot of people, one of their ambitions in life is to be buried in a Louis Copeland suit.

In any business, teamwork is hugely important, and so is
achieving a business culture in which people can work well.

I n business, making mistakes is inevitable. It's part of the learning
process. In fact, I would say that, if you are not prepared to make
mistakes, you won't prosper. In my case, I've made plenty of
mistakes. I've bought suits in colours that people didn't want to buy,
and I've purchased styles that turned out to be too adventurous, and
done other things that, in retrospect, I shouldn't have. 'Nothing
ventured, nothing gained', is a useful proverb to bear in mind.

There can also be times when circumstances conspire against you. I
remember one time about 25 years ago, we were doing some
construction work on the shop in Capel Street that was supposed to
have cost IR£15,000 and, before I knew it, we had run up to IR£70,000
or IR£80,000, and the banks started insisting that we sort it out.

Marketing is hugely important, and I use every chance I see
to get our name – Louis Copeland – out there.

O ne piece of advice I would give to young people starting in
business is that they should work on maintaining a good
relationship with the bank. Things can always go wrong, and
there will be times when one needs support, and these are the times
when this will pay off. I remember, during that period, that we had to
be careful about writing cheques, to ensure that there was the money
there to cover them.

It's important to plan, rather than entering into things willy-nilly,
and then having to deal with the consequences. If plans are in place,
the banks generally will help. Young people starting out in business
benefit hugely from talking to more experienced people, and most
people who are successful in their own business are happy to share
their knowledge and insights. Speaking for myself, I love helping
people and I'm always prepared to offer advice when I can. So are

most of the business people I know: Padraig Ó Céidigh, for example, would stand on his head to help out.

One piece of advice I would give to young people starting in business is that they should work on maintaining a good relationship with the bank.

M arketing is hugely important, and I use every chance I see to get our name, Louis Copeland, out there. I am sometimes asked how I manage to get so much publicity for the shop, and the fact is that one has to work hard to get one's name out there. For every 10 phone calls I make, I score with one. The main thing is making those calls in the first place – this is something that is often overlooked.

Another area where Irish business people often fall down is in the area of caring for staff. Managers can forget to 'hug the huggers', as I say; in other words, to listen to, and to take care of the needs of, the people who take care of the customers. It is hugely important that staff members are happy in their work because, when they are not, customers can sense it, and it has a negative impact on their experience of the business

Business people need to put themselves into their customers' position and ask how they would like to be treated in those circumstances.

A s I mentioned, my father was my original teacher and mentor in business, but throughout one's working life, everyone's a teacher, from other retailers and manufacturers to the customers. Now that we stock so much off-the-peg merchandise, we get in items from designers such as Canali and Brioni. We carry all the big brands in Europe and, at Louis Copeland, we learn from them all the time. I travel a lot during the buying periods, in spring and autumn; that's about a month of travel every year, and I must say that I enjoy it, and use every trip as a learning experience, although one year tends to roll into another.

I have met a lot of interesting people through work, and a lot of prominent Irish men buy their suits at Louis Copeland. Bertie Ahern, for example, always bought two sets of suits from us: one for when he had put on some weight, and one for when he lost it. Dressing smartly has never been his priority, but I think it would be fair to refer to him as the 'most improved politician' with respect to clothes! One problem with him has been that he sometimes wears the 'skinny Bertie' clothes when he is big, and *vice versa*.

I do enjoy seeing people dressed in our clothes, and looking well, and when I see Pat Kenny, Mark Little, Mark Cagney, Brian Dobson, or any of the men who wear Louis Copeland on the television or in the papers in our clothes, and looking well, it does feel very good to know that I dressed them; it's great for the ego, and that's the sort of thing that keeps me going.

Our business is done through the seat of the pants – no pun intended! It's important to keep on top of changes in society, and to keep one's eyes open for opportunities. For example, recently I saw the opportunity to open a small satellite shop in the IFSC, and thought, "Well, if Mohammed can't come to the mountain let the mountain go to Mohammed". By now, we have a number of shops, including the original shop on Capel Street, and the Pembroke Street shop, which is run by my brother Adrian. There's also a shop on Wicklow Street, one in Galway and one in Dublin Airport. More recently, we've started the Hugo Boss franchise in the Dundrum Shopping Centre in Dublin, and the first stand-alone Gant shop in Ireland, also in the Dundrum shopping centre. As for bringing the Louis Copeland brand outside Ireland, I have no current plans, although in the future, who knows? Maybe I'll leave that to the younger generation; as I said, my son Louis is already in the business, so when my daughter joins the team, perhaps she could start a ladies' wear branch; we could call it 'Louise Copeland'!

In business, making mistakes is inevitable.
It's part of the learning process.

What I enjoy most about my work is meeting all walks of life. I love meeting people; I don't care who they are or where they come from. If I hadn't gone into the rag trade, I think I would have enjoyed working in a hotel or front-of-house in a restaurant. What I like best is meeting people and making sure they're happy. Fortunately for me, customer service is the most important element of my business. In fact, I think that for *any* business to survive today it is absolutely essential to have good customer service, and also that hard work and great customer service will stand a business in good stead, regardless of the general economic environment. My motto is 'do unto others as you'd have them do unto you'. Business people need to put themselves into their customers' position and ask how they would like to be treated in those circumstances. Nobody is going to get it right all the time, and of course we don't, but we do try to give good customer service. By and large, it has paid off very well. In 1998, for example, we won *Retailer of the Year* in the Drapers' Awards. The competition was open to everyone in the business in Ireland and Great Britain, and we were the first Irish business to win, which was wonderful, especially as we were up against organisations like Harrods and Selfridges. There was a lot of media attention at the time, which is good; I'm not shy when it comes to getting media attention!

> *People with natural talent and ability will always do well,*
> *but I feel strongly that a good education is*
> *an excellent background, in providing*
> *an outline of knowledge and understanding.*

Iirish business culture has changed a lot in recent years. For one thing, young people in business today have no direct experience of more difficult times. I often hear them saying, "Oh, I'm very busy, I'm very stressed", and looking very glum. When I think back about the more difficult days, I can't help but remind them that the stress of being very busy is better than the stress of being very quiet. If you think about it, being stressed about being too busy should be a cause for delight! At the same time, Irish people today are very entrepreneurial, very 'get up and go'. For a lot of them, money is the biggest motivating factor. They want to make lots of it! For me, assuming that I am earning enough to live comfortably, money isn't the main thing. What I love, and what is always my goal, is achieving good service and knowing that when people walk out of my shop they are happy, and they will recommend the shop to their friends.

At the moment, my fear is that, with all the shopping centres and retail units that are opening, we will soon be like every other country in Europe and simply have too many shops, with the result that there will be casualties along the way. Again, the only real way to combat this eventuality is to focus on customer service, and to remember Feargal Quinn's boomerang symbol, and how we can make sure people return by giving them what they want and need.

In any business, teamwork is hugely important, and so is achieving a business culture in which people can work well. A lot of our staff start out as messenger boys and come up through the ranks. At Louis Copeland, we generally see our customers more as friends than clients, which ensures a good, happy environment. This is something that our staff learns about by observing and becoming part of our business culture rather than through formal training. Of course, we have managers, but there's no 'boss'. Everybody works, everybody pulls their weight. It might be a bit of a cliché, but teamwork is absolutely crucial.

I think that hard work and great customer service
will stand a business in good stead,
regardless of the general economic environment.

Of the Irish business people whom I know personally and in other ways, I'm a great admirer of Feargal Quinn in particular. So far as I am concerned, he is one of the best retailers in the country, and anyone could learn a huge amount from him with respect to customer service. He takes care of the finishing touches, and he runs a fantastic business in general. Conversely, I have to say I also admire Michael O'Leary as a businessman, although customer service is not really the selling point of Ryanair. He is someone who certainly does not take any prisoners! In fact, if any aspiring business person wanted a good way to make progress, they could do a lot worse than by taking couple of leaves from Feargal Quinn's and couple of leaves from Michael O'Leary's book; that would be quite a combination!

Irish people today are very entrepreneurial,
very 'get up and go'.

A chieving a balance between life and work is important but, if it was not for my wife, I would never take any time off; I would work 20 hours a day. I like working and, if you like what you do, life is one long holiday! I work six or even seven days a week, but I do take short breaks. Every two months or so, my wife and I go off for five or six days; I couldn't cope with longer, because I would get bored. Mary is the homemaker in our family. She makes sure that we are all fed and watered and looked after in general, and that is very important. I would not have a successful business today if I didn't have the comforts of home and the support that she offers.

Somebody once asked me where I found motivation to keep going. To tell the truth, I think what drives me most is the fear of insecurity and the memory of difficult times when it seemed as though things were falling on top of me. That's what makes me get up in the morning and keep going.

I love meeting people;
I don't care who they are or where they come from.

4

DENIS DESMOND

Denis Desmond is the founder and CEO of MCD, Ireland's largest concert promoters, an organisation that started in the 1970s with such greats as Thin Lizzy, went on to work with bands including U2, Celine Dion, Oasis and Westlife and now brings the world's finest artists to headline events such as Slane and Oxegen, the music festival.

MCD is also deeply involved in promoting theatre and other spectacular events that have all played a leading role in turning Ireland into one of Europe's finest cultural destinations.

MCD owns an extensive portfolio of entertainment venues including the Olympia and Gaiety theatres, as well as an interest in London's Mean Fiddler.

A SCÉIL FHÉIN

I was born in 1953 and raised in Cork city. My father was a butcher and, when not in school, my time was spent working in his shop. I attended the Presentation Boys' school in Cork and, while most boys my age were into sports, I spent my time listening to music and devouring music magazines. I continued my education in University College Cork, study civil engineering, and qualified as a civil engineer in 1970.

At 17, Joe O'Herlihy (U2's sound engineer), who at the time was working with a Cork band called Sleepy Hollow. I became Sleepy Hollow's agent. In those days, the Cork music scene was very much dominated by Rory Gallagher, who took Sleepy Hollow under his wing, and arranged for them to play support when he toured the UK. Soon after, I began to take on other bands, such as Gaslight, and booking shows in the Arcadia Ballroom in Cork together with a woman called Elvira Butler, who now runs Reekus Records.

On completing my degree, I started working as an engineer, initially in Cork and then in various locations in the United Kingdom. However, my passion for music continued, and my weekends and evenings were spent on the phone booking bands and organising events.

In those days, the business of concert promoting was very much in its infancy. The pioneers were Jim Aiken, Pat Egan and Oliver Barry. Pat Egan was Ireland's answer to Richard Branson, owning record shops that stocked rock music as opposed to the showbands that dominated Ireland. He was also a writer for *Spotlight* magazine, which was the leading music publication at the time. He was very helpful to me; I used to write to him for advice and he was always generous in giving it.

Because the whole scene was nascent, it was hard to make any money from it, so working in the area full-time would still have been difficult. From the UK, I started putting bands onto the university circuit in Ireland in collaboration with the universities' social secretaries, Eamonn McCann in Belfast, or Padraic Boran in Cork. Eamonn and myself started promoting concerts. Around this time, U2 were beginning to arrive on the scene, and there was a period when they were much bigger in Cork than in Dublin, attracting 1,600 Cork students as opposed to just 500 in Dublin.

As U2 got bigger, Joe and myself began supplying them with equipment, which in those days all fitted in the back of a Transit van. A new era had started, with bands carrying more equipment and more international bands started to play Ireland.

I remember doing Pink Floyd, with very few people turning up to see them. This was the era when Punk was emerging, with bands like The Stranglers, The Sex Pistols, The Clash, Dr Feelgood, and many more. Eamonn and myself were very much the rookies on the block, taking on the larger promoters, all in a bit of healthy competition.

In the late 1970s, we got a chance to work with Thin Lizzy, who were being promoted in Dublin and Belfast by Jim Aiken. However, nobody was doing regional shows. We booked them into venues all over the country, our first big tour. Rock and roll had officially come to town.

I think if you want to start in a business, you still have to start at the bottom and work your way up.

In 1981, I was faced with a choice to make: either I took up promoting as a full-time business, or I continued my career as an engineer. I was at a crossroads but, in the end, I chose to quit my job as an engineer and go full-time as a music promoter. I returned to Ireland, coinciding with the first concert to be held at Slane Castle.

So, in 1981, we did the first concert at Slane Castle. Thin Lizzy topped the bill and U2, among others, played support. The following year, the Rolling Stones were playing in Leixlip with another promoter, and we decided we would try and get them to do Slane. In the event, we did persuade them to move to Slane, but Jim Aiken promoted the show. In Dublin, we were organising shows in places like the RDS Simmonscourt, the Olympic Ballroom, the Stardust and the SFX Centre on Upper Sheridan Street; this was still long before the days of The Point.

Throughout the 1980s, with Eamonn McCann as my partner in crime, we were organising shows for U2, Bon Jovi, REM, Def Leppard, Spandau Ballet, Frankie goes to Hollywood, Eurhythmics, Echo & the Bunnymen, ABC, Simple Minds, Thompson Twins, Big Country, etc, culminating at the end of the decade with the first *Féile* concert in Semple Stadium in Thurles. That event actually came about in large part because the stadium had a huge debt, as opposed to a desire to hold a rock concert. Thankfully, Michael Lowry had the vision to let it happen. In those days, there was still a widespread feeling that big rock concerts were not something to be desired and that they brought nothing but trouble. *Féile* did very well; however, there were some logistic issues: the campsite was half a mile away from the stadium, and people were partying in town, which meant that people had to be controlled in three separate areas. It is easier when a festival is contained, so we tried to move to Mondello in County Kildare, which would provide better facilities. Some of the residents took us to court, and the court ruled that, from now on, we would have to have planning permission to put up a temporary stage. That year, we ended up having to move to Cork and, despite the fantastic line-up, including the Stone Roses and Kylie Minogue, we lost a fortune, thanks to the stream of headlines saying 'Festival in doubt'.

In the mid-90s, Slane suffered from similar planning issues and, for a while, concerts were not held there either. At around the same time, I started to promote in Scotland, together with Stuart Clumpas, setting up the 'T in the Park' festival, which is still going strong to this day and is an integral part of the Scottish cultural scene.

The difference in attitude between the Irish and the Scottish authorities was incredible. In Scotland, we were offered grants, while in Ireland we were being threatened with prosecution on a continuous basis. It was absurd. Business was booming, and more and more bands wanted to come and perform in Ireland, but finding venues for them was very difficult, as objectors kept jumping on the bandwagon, while big venues like the RDS were restricted to a small number of events every year. Fortunately, The Point had opened in 1988, which meant that there was at least one sizeable venue that was welcoming to large acts. We were a little frustrated at the time, in general, because we could see just how much potential there was for music business in Ireland, but found ourselves limited by the lack of venues and the absurd planning restrictions. Thankfully, we now have a system of licensing, like in the UK, which is a much quicker process. Bertie Ahern introduced licensing, and thereafter the authorities accepted that running festivals is a *bona fide* business that is part of our culture and to be encouraged rather than restricted. Concerts and festivals bring huge numbers of tourists to Ireland, and add to Ireland's reputation as a centre of culture.

> *Business is really about contacts.*
> *So, for anybody who's starting up, it's all about the*
> *contacts. The address book and the contacts.*

Another big change that we have seen in recent years is that the demographic of audiences has shifted a lot. A large majority of ticket buyers are still in their late teens and early 20s, but we now also do events for people aged from eight to 80. If you go to an Avril Lavigne concert, the average age will be 11; however, if you were to attend a Neil Diamond performance, the average age will be closer to 60.

Our business, as a whole, has grown enormously, and facilities and venues have become progressively better and better. For bands and performers, live shows have become much more important. In the 1980s and 1990s, bands typically toured to sell records, whereas now they bring out records to promote their tours, which are where the real money is being made. Promoters often work with a band from the relatively early days, starting with live shows in clubs. When an act is good, people will come back to see them.

> *I think that … we have the right attitude, we've never been*
> *afraid. We've always said, "We'll go for that".*

P romotion has always been a very risky business; that comes with the territory. There will often be shows where 40,000 people will turn up, but we've needed 50,000 in order to break-even. Even when the band plays really well and the crowd is happy, money has been lost. We have to book events 12 months ahead, and six months can be a long time for a band's career to change. One minute they can be as hot as they come, only to be yesterday's news by the time the gig is on. Radio is one of the factors that are enormously influential as to who is going to be the next big thing. Bands need radio play. When I started, there was just RTÉ, and that was it. Nowadays, radio stations are more abundant and diverse and, thanks in part to the availability of Internet downloads, records have become much more affordable. Many things are much cheaper now than they used to be, and it has become easier to take initiative in a whole range of areas.

One of the areas where MCD has been able to make progress has been in recycling. We started this in Scotland, with T in the Park, where it was called 'Greening the Festival', and we actually won a few awards for it, which was great! Now, we are working on making Oxegen more environmentally-friendly by providing recycling services. Customers have become more aware and discerning in most ways. In the past, people would buy whatever tickets were available, because there were so few concerts on. Now, there is so much to choose from that people can afford to be discerning, and they pick and choose, and are more concerned with issues such as the environment.

Along the way, I started to branch out from just focusing on promoting rock concerts. While promoting is exciting, it is also very high risk, and after moving *Féile* to Cork, and both Slane and *Féile* having the same planning issues, I nearly lost everything. On the verge of ruin, I swore that I would never allow myself to be put in this position again.

I bought the Olympia and the Gaiety theatres in Dublin, and become involved in theatre shows. We also branched out into children's entertainment, such as Disney on Ice. MCD has become an all-round entertainment business. We have also expanded into the UK, apart from the T in the Park, which has continued to run successfully in Scotland. Together with local partners, I got involved with the V Festival in Chelmsford and Stafford, which has about 16 venues. A few years later, I purchased with Live Nation the Mean Fiddler Group.

I also have a record label, which has been involved over the years with bands including The Stunning, The Saw Doctors, Mary Coughlin, Sinéad O'Connor, and Rodrigo y Gabriella.

It was around this time that I became one of the founder shareholders in Today FM, with John McLoughlin and Moya Doherty, and later sold the station in 2002. We also back Phantom music station, along with Paul McGuinness, and we teamed up with Abrakebabra founder Graeme Beere, who has now branched out into other food areas, including The Bagel Factory, Yo Sushi!, and the Gourmet Burger Kitchen.

"Hey!" So we learned a lesson, but it was
an interesting time.

Over the years, there have been plenty of instances where we've had to take a step back in order to continue to go forward, and when we've been successful, but not as much as we would have liked. For example, our record label started off doing really well and then, although we had some great performers like The Saw Doctors and Sharon Shannon, it didn't provide us with the return we might have hoped for.

In the United Kingdom, we teamed up with Dan Robinson, formerly of Stiff Records, and released The Saw Doctors, selling 50,000 copies of their album, which was fantastic. Then Warner Brothers came in and offered us big money to sign the label, which we did. The idea was that this would help us to go global, but it didn't work out that way. We found that we were losing control of artists with whom we had had great success. Warners were changing everything and, in the end, we paid them back the advance and got the label back. Currently, we have a record label called Rubyworks, which is building nicely.

We opened a venue in New York called Spirit, initially without a local partner, and it didn't go according to plan at all. The property was great, so we did well out of it anyway, but I won't be rushing back to the United States, and the knowledge that local partners are essential to any enterprise overseas was strongly reinforced.

*I'm in the wonderful position that I wake up and
I look forward to the day.*

T he great strength we have at MCD is our team. I work with a
great bunch of people, some of whom have been with the
company for more than 20 years and who have seen the
business grow and flourish. About 15 years ago, we started our own
in-house press and marketing company, which was managed by Justin
Green. We do pay attention to continuous learning in the organisation,
in terms of attending a lot of industry conferences in Los Angeles,
London and so forth. These events are great for learning opportunities
and for networking, and they are where all the bookers and promoters
meet up and see up-and-coming artists.

We are also part of the European Health & Safety Committee,
which is hugely important. Obviously, there are lots of health and
safety issues associated with concerts, from policing to alcohol intake,
although I have seen how, over the years, Irish concert goers have
gradually become more and more responsible with respect to alcohol
intake and consumption. I don't think that they get the credit they
deserve. Ireland leads the pack from a health and safety point of view.

Outside my own field of concert promotion, I find that there are a
lot of business people in Ireland to admire, and I have to say that I am
very impressed by the work of some of the great property developers
and speculators, who worked through the difficult times in the 1980s,
when the economy was in a very bad situation and interest rates
terribly high, but held onto their vision and came out at the other end.
I also have huge admiration for the people who have taken their
business to a global level. Within the indigenous music industry, look
at the phenomenal success that is Paul McGuinness, and the band U2.
From one of the smaller countries in the world, we have the biggest
band in the world, managed by a man who has been with them for
three decades. The Rolling Stones can't claim to have had the same
management all the way through their career. I also have a lot of
respect for Moya Doherty, who is the director of Tyrone Productions,
and producer of *Riverdance*. I also have respect for entrepreneurs who
say "Yes" to whatever challenges they are faced with, and run the risk.

I think Irish people in general, to be honest, Irish people and
Irish entrepreneurs as such, to me have no fear.
I think that's the great thing about us.

W hile, obviously, the scope and range has changed a lot over the years, what I enjoy about the business has remained essentially the same. I still get a huge buzz out of working with bands, and seeing them grow, as I did with Oasis, from playing small clubs, to a crowd of 600 people, to playing massive venues to 80,000 people. The first show we arranged with Robbie Williams was held in the Olympia to just a few hundred, and later to 120,000 in Phoenix Park. It is truly incredible to be involved with a band from the early stages, and to see a band grow and conquer. Being a part of that is phenomenal, and it's something I hope to continue.

I think that Irish businesspeople are fantastic, smart and motivated. They are fearless and unsurpassed at selling themselves and their abilities. Business is about confidence; knocking on people's doors, going in there and saying, "We can do this". That's why Ireland has done so well; it is one of our gifts. We accept challenge and risk. An opportunity has to be analysed and discussed, but the fact is that sometimes risks have to be made, and money has to be lost in the short term, so as to complete long-term gains.

My wife probably would say I work too hard, as would my children, but I enjoy doing what I do! I'm in the wonderful position that I get to wake up every morning and look forward to doing what I'm doing – and I'm happy with that. Having said that, I don't work at as frantic a pace as I once did, and I do go on holidays with my family to Spain, but I'm never really unreachable. I'm just not one of those people who can take off on vacation and say, "See you in three weeks". I am incredibly grateful for modern technology, as it makes it possible for me to go away without being completely out of touch. Blackberries, or 'crackberries' as my wife so affectionately calls them, make it possible for me to relax and still be clued in. I still look back on the great days when we were touring around Ireland with Thin Lizzy, and when we were still out there knocking on people's doors to arrange venues, like when Eamonn McCann got the ball rolling at

Slane by knocking on Henry Mount Charles' door. I have enjoyed business since the beginning, despite all the ups and downs I have faced. I would find having to switch off completely terribly stressful!

So you have to have the thrill that you get out of doing it and actually putting on the event and looking and saying, "This is good". The success and the money actually follow.

My advice to future promoters is this: promotion is a very high-risk business, one is financially exposed, and it's not easy to deal with the risk if that passion and drive isn't there. There has to be that element of thrill when an event comes off well. I don't think that anybody who gets involved in the business does so for the money, as the risks are too high. For an 18-year-old to come to me and say "I want to promote a band" is tough at the moment, so most of them start working with promoters as junior bookers so that they can learn and build their reputation. Some people who started out with us like that are now are competitors, which is fantastic. Who knows, one day it could be you!

5

DECLAN GANLEY

Declan Ganley is a leading Irish and European entrepreneur, and founder of wireless broadband and cable TV networks, in western, central and eastern Europe: namely, Broadnet, which built wireless networks in 10 countries, including Germany, France, Spain and the UK; and Cabeltel, with an extensive cable multi-media network in Eastern Europe.

From 1991 to 1997, Declan founded and built what became the largest privately-held forestry business in the former Soviet Union, before selling the business in 1997. Declan is Chairman and CEO of Rivada Networks, designing and deploying public safety communications networks for government customers in the United States and Europe. He is an advisor on 'technology and terrorism' to the Club De Madrid group of international heads of government.

He is a member of the Futures Group of the Irish Government's Information Society Commission, and he is also a member of Britain's Royal Institute of International Affairs. He is head of policy for the Brussels-based pan-European entrepreneurs association 'Entrepreneurs for Growth / Europe's 500', and also serves in the Irish Army Reserve.

His writings on transatlantic and European affairs have been published by the Foreign Policy Research Institute and he has authored numerous reports for governments on communications policy. He is Chairman of the Forum on Public Safety in Europe & North America, the reports of which have been requested by the United States Senate Foreign Relations Committee and the European Parliament.

He has received several awards for business achievement, including the *Outstanding Irish Young Person of the Year Award* 2001 for entrepreneurial accomplishment and the JCI Ireland *Entrepreneur of the Year* 2005.

He is married to Delia, a native of New York City, and has four children.

He is chairman of the Libertas Institute, which states that its aims are to initiate and provoke enlightened discussion on the European Union, its relevance to its Member States and peoples and its role in world affairs, having regard to our shared values of peace, democracy, individual liberty and free markets. The Libertas organisation has been accredited by many as the primary driver behind the defeat of the Lisbon Treaty referendum in Ireland in 2008.

A SCÉIL FHÉIN

I was born and brought up through my primary school years in London, because my parents, like so many others, were economic migrants. Both from the West of Ireland, they travelled to London in the early 1960s to find work. My mother is from Dooega on Achill Island, and my dad from a little village called Lisheenaheitia near Glenamaddy. On both sides of the family, there was a tradition of emigration, as was the case for most families in the West. Although they had come home, my grandparents and great-grandparents had all emigrated for a time and, in fact, one set of great-grandparents married in Boston and came back to Ireland through Manchester. My parents met in The Galtymore in Cricklewood, in London. They married in 1967, and I was born a year later in Watford, where my parents had moved to start a family, always with the intention of eventually returning to Ireland.

In our house, whenever anyone talked about 'home', they were referring to Ireland and, specifically, to west of the Shannon. We all lived from one visit home to the next and, even though I was being brought up in North London, I always had a very acute awareness of my Irishness, probably more so than many Irish kids in Ireland did; being a minority made even a child ultra-aware of their identity, as there was always someone, somewhere, trying to deny you of it. The primary school I went to was Catholic and largely attended by Irish kids, along with some Italians and a small number of Catholic West Indians and Indians. Our area, St. Michael's Parish in Garston, Watford, had a great community life and, all in all, it was a stimulating environment to be in as a child.

All the summers of my childhood were spent with grandparents in Achill Island or near Glenamaddy, and they were wonderful times; fishing in Achill, working on the bog or saving hay in both places, spending summers in Dooega barefoot, as my parents and grandparents had done before me, and helping out on the farm. In my early years in Lisheen, there were just three tractors in the whole village, which were called on when there was a need, but people were still commonly using the ass and cart for daily chores. In Achill, too, I remember using the creels on the ass to draw out the turf from the bog and then going up the dirt road to my grandparents' house. It was the most wonderful thing. Of my four grandparents, only one grandmother could drive and had a car, and life was all about what was happening in the village. My grandparents' house in Lisheen in particular at times was something of a focal point in the village; my family all played and enjoyed traditional music, and I have many early memories of sitting in the parlour with my grandfather playing the fiddle and my uncles playing their instruments. I can see now that what I was witnessing was the very end of an era in Ireland and I feel extremely lucky to have experienced it. As each summer drew to a close, it was as if a cloud came over us. Every holiday ended with tears as the Volkswagen roof-rack would be loaded for the lonely return to North Wall or Dun Laoghaire and the boat back to England.

Our family finally returned to Ireland for good when I was almost 13, and I attended Coláiste Seosaimh in Glenamaddy, now known as the Glenamaddy Community School. In those days, it was run by the Sisters of Mercy. They were phenomenal; fantastic teachers and extraordinarily dedicated women who committed their lives to education, together with some very talented lay teachers. We students were the central focus of everything that they did. I didn't know it at the time, but I found out afterwards that the nuns used to pool the salary that they got and used it to subsidise books and supplies for the school, as well as cleaning the schools after hours by themselves. It is dreadful, now, to see all the criticism that is levelled at the religious orders, while they just don't defend themselves. I have nothing but great things to say about all of the religious I encountered in school, and the enormity of the value of the sacrifices they made to provide world-class education in a most challenging environment.

I would question the extent to which entrepreneurship can be taught. It is like music. You can teach someone how to play the guitar, but can you teach someone to play like Eric Clapton? I don't think so.

I did my Leaving Cert in 1987. I didn't go to university; I went straight to London instead. Everyone was leaving Ireland at the time. Leaving wasn't just something you wanted to do; it was something you *had* to do. I got a job on a building site the first day I arrived, and I also worked in a bar at night.

However, from the very start, I knew I wanted to do something in business, so as soon as possible I got a job in the city as an office 'go-for' with an insurance company. I had to serve tea and coffee, but I got to wear a suit. I spent as much time as I could reading whatever I could get my hands on, especially about communications and aerospace technology.

To cut a long story short, I came up with an idea for putting together insurance packages for commercial satellite launches on Soviet boosters instead of Western launch platforms. The space shuttle Challenger had blown up the year before, in 1986. When I pitched the idea to a partner at that firm, he thought it was interesting, and told me to go and research it. I got out the *Yellow Pages* and looked under 'S' for 'Soviet'. The Soviet Trade Delegation was listed, so I rang them and asked for an appointment, which I got. It was bizarre. There I was, at just 19, pitching an idea to people who seemed to take me seriously, much to my own surprise! I ended up organising for a group to travel to Moscow in January 1988, to meet Glavkosmos, the Soviet Space Agency. They signed a contract to launch communication satellites, which was subsequently shelved because industry lobbyists intervened with the US government; the satellites in question would have been US commercial satellites and there were potential issues with technology transfer regulations.

I left my first job in the City after a short period, and started up on my own with an office on the Kingsbury Road in London, in a building called Knightsbridge House. That sounds very grand, but the office was just a very basic room above a car spray shop and, because I couldn't afford both an office and a flat, I also slept there in a sleeping bag, and had meals at my aunts and uncles in London when ever I could.

My first employee was a wonderful guy for whom I had worked as a steel fixer before getting the office job. He had gone out of the business in the late 1980s property slump in the UK. I met him in a bar in Rayners Lane one evening and he told me that he would like to help me. I couldn't pay him anything, but he was anxious to have something challenging to do. With his help, using the contacts that I had made in Russia, I was asked to organise an exhibition of Soviet metal alloys and ceramics, so that these products would get some exposure in the West. In 1989, I organised SovMat 90, an exhibition to be held the following year at the Institute of Metals in London.

That led to my becoming involved in the export of aluminium from Krasnoyarsk in Siberia through Riga in Latvia, which was still in the Soviet Union at that time. In 1991, Latvia declared its independence from Russia. I had got to know some of the members of the Latvian Popular Front, the Latvian independence movement. These were people who were young, idealistic, driven risk-takers, who risked their lives for the independence of their country, and it was inspirational to be in their company. I was appointed as advisor for Foreign Economic Affairs Policy to the new governing authorities. What we all lacked in experience (and that was a lot in my case) we made up for in enthusiasm! I ended up helping to put together a timber exporting business out of Latvia, to generate foreign currency income.

We started exporting timber in small quantities and learned by trial and error. That went well, so the quantities increased until it reached a point where we decided that we needed to extend our footprint and move into areas where there was a greater supply upstream. We ended up privatising 28 wood-processing facilities, saw mills, in north-western Russia, primarily in the Vologda region. We took out leases on substantial tracts of forest and privatised them. I ran that business until August 1997, when it was sold on.

The work was gruelling, often travelling through the night on old Soviet trains and experiencing the brutal climate of that part of the world, but it was a great experience and fascinating to see both the opportunities opening up with increasing freedom and the absolute destruction wrought by Communism, which had suppressed the people, massacred millions and left scars that, when I was there, were still very raw. Churches had been destroyed and monasteries turned into prisons, I visited them, the gutted shells of what Russian culture once was, their wreckage left as testimony to the price of unaccountable, dictatorial government, out of control and unleashed on its own people. Ronald Reagan had been completely accurate when he labelled Soviet Communism the 'Evil Empire'. What was inspirational was the fact that the spirit of the Russians was tremendous; they had survived Communism. I remember that many Russians used to talk about how Russia needed a Pinochet. Well, they've got one now, in Putin, so that's a lesson in how you should be careful what you wish for! Although, having said that, in Russia, he is very popular.

It was a great experience and fascinating to see
both the opportunities opening up with increasing freedom
and the absolute destruction wrought by Communism.

While all of this was going on, I also spent some time in the Middle East and Far East, exploring opportunities. Although I had got involved with forestry almost by accident, telecommunications remained an interest, so I set up an engineering company in the UK, and we put together a consortium to bid for the second GSM license here in Ireland. In the event, it was awarded to ESAT. Through that effort, I had put together a competent management team that really knew the wireless industry. This lead in turn to setting up Broadnet, with the intention of getting licenses for wireless broadband. In the 1990s, broadband was still very new. We successfully won licenses in a highly competitive environment across 10 countries in Europe, beating the likes of France Telecom and Deutsch Telecom. We had the top 42 cities in Germany and the top cities in France. We created a network in Spain, and won licenses in Norway, Austria, the Czech Republic, Switzerland, Portugal, in Greater London and the UK. In fact, the only country where we applied and did not win a license was Ireland which, as an Irishman, was a little annoying—or would have been if I had possessed the time to dwell on it. Broadnet went on to be acquired by Comcast and I went on to set up a dotcom business called Adornis.com.

Adornis, a jewellery retailer, was very high profile at the time; *Time* magazine labelled it 'Luxury Central on the Web'. We were on the *Forbes* list of the top 20 websites in the world, every month for nine months. I had put together a superstar management team, with people like the former president and former gemologist of Tiffany's and the former head of jewellery from Saks. It was rock 'n' roll and the overheads were high, but the business wasn't making enough money! Dotcoms were all going bust, and when the time came for me to get out my chequebook and write another cheque, I realised that I had to pull the plug. Because the business had been very high profile, leaving it behind was very hard to do. In some ways, it would have been easier to leave something in place and carry on; initially, that's what I was going to do but walking away was the right thing to do.

Following the closure of Adornis, I got involved in Bulgaria. We set up a fibre-optic ring around the country and acquired a number of local cable television networks. We built that up, sold it on to a group of investors, and set up Rivada Networks, based on emergency telecommunications lessons learned in the wake of September 11th.

As almost everyone alive knows, the attack on the World Trade Center had huge resonance around the world. It also had personal resonance in our family. My wife's brother-in-law was a New York fire-fighter, and a business owned by my wife's family was run out of the World Trade Center, so the attack really was a seminal moment for us all. I knew from my involvement in the Army Reserve in Ireland that our communication systems were appalling, but I had assumed that that level of inefficiency was unique to here. After 9/11, it was obvious that the same issues were a problem even in the United States. This suggested both a need and an opportunity, and prompted me to get a team together and to set up Rivada Networks to fill that gap. While the need for our services is global, we decided to start in the US, with the idea of taking our services to Europe once we had established a track record and a customer base in the US, as we have now done.

Entrepreneurship is often misunderstood;
people often see it as limited to just business and
money-making, while I would see it as the creative and
successful harnessing of risk against what others perceive
to be overwhelming odds; properly calculated, smart
assumption of risk, executed for high reward.

One of the salient features of American culture is the way that Americans embrace entrepreneurship. It was an American President, Calvin Coolidge, who said "The business of America is business". The first time I raised money, at 19 or 20, I went to the US and managed to talk some New York businessmen into investing in Russia. Can you imagine a kid of that age doing something of the sort in Europe, especially at that time? You wouldn't get in the door! The American way of doing business is all about embracing risk-taking, which is the spirit of entrepreneurship.

Entrepreneurship is often misunderstood; people often see it as limited to just business and money-making, while I would see it as the creative and successful harnessing of risk against what others perceive to be overwhelming odds; properly calculated, smart assumption of risk, executed for high reward. Entrepreneurship exists in all fields. There's no reason why this spirit of risk-taking should be unique to America and, in fact, entrepreneurship is growing apace in other places, too. In Ireland, it was suppressed for a long time, but there's absolutely nothing to stop Irish people from being hugely successful. Look at the demographic that makes up entrepreneurs in the US; lots of them are Irish or of Irish descent. They just needed to go to a new environment to realise their skills. These were people who went to America and, without losing their Irish identity, enthusiastically embraced being Americans, and the very idea of the Republic. During the American Civil War, many of them fought as Americans and as Irishmen.

In Ireland, the disposition of society was averse to risk-taking for a long, long time. Look at Irish history! For centuries, risk-taking outside a few narrowly-defined areas was not generally rewarded and nobody engaged in it unless they wanted to be a martyr. What happened to the risk-takers in 1798, for example? They went down with the first volley of shot from the redcoats. Again, look at the leaders in 1916; what a sterling example of entrepreneurship, and they certainly weren't doing it for the money!

Things have changed vastly in Ireland since the 1980s. It has ceased to be necessary for the Irish to leave Ireland in order to excel in their field. Now, we have a whole generation of young and youngish – speaking as someone who has just turned 40 – entrepreneurs, who are out there doing remarkable things. Some are well-known and there are others who are never heard about, quietly and humbly doing great things. They provide a sharp contrast to our political class, which in spite of the varnish, remains firmly in the old school of thinking, even though some politicians may be young, looking askance on risk-taking, entrepreneurship and out-of-the-box thinking.

As well as a change in attitude in areas outside politics, entrepreneurship in Ireland has benefitted from changes in technology. Before telecommunications and travel were more accessible, people would leave the country, do well, and stay away, maybe coming back as old people to spend a weekend in Ashford Castle. Mine was the first generation that really benefitted from being able to travel easily. When I originally emigrated to London, I met more people from Glenamaddy in London than I would have at home. Then, after a while, Virgin and then Ryanair started flying more often and more cheaply to Ireland and suddenly it was feasible to go home for the weekend or to live in Ireland, knowing that travelling out would be easy. While, in previous generations, a huge amount of talent was lost to emigration, now people come back. The talent is there, and it has become acceptable to embrace risk in general society.

Unfortunately, despite the massive wealth of talent available in Ireland, entrepreneurship and innovation are held back by our political class, which is sadly outdated. The government is trailing far behind even the civil service. Many of the civil servants I have met have been great, talented people of excellent calibre. Our education system produced highly trained people, many of whom chose to go into the civil service rather than business; hopefully, we will be able to maintain this high standard over the next 20 years. At the same time, we all have to confront the serious problem, with profound repercussions for business, which is the fact that our politicians are still operating in a very old-fashioned way, with no meaningful opposition at all, especially since the PDs failed to make any change. Until now, nobody has bothered to tinker with the *status quo*, we have been rewarding mediocrity, growing paralysis was being mislabelled 'consensus', consensus in our case ended up being the very lowest common denominator . You get to the polling booth and vote for one or the other, because you've made friends, or you know the person who is running or you've got involved in your local Cumann and want to be an active citizen. But the closer you get to seeing government close up, the more obvious it is that you're looking at a cardio-vascular system whose arteries are not just clogged, but caked and calcified. They are like rocks. It is not just broken, it is totally, totally screwed from the bottom up. There's no fresh blood getting into the system at all because it is not being let in.

Irish business people have managed, not because of much that our government has ever done, but in spite of it. In recent years, Irish government has become essentially a stamp duty collection operation, collecting the stamp duty and doling it out. The economy is having difficulties now, but the writing has been on the wall since 2000.

People who are going to be successful as entrepreneurs
will have a track record of risk-taking
and they will have hunger, enthusiasm, raw intelligence,
willingness to learn and street-smarts.

To support Ireland and entrepreneurship in Ireland, we need to churn out a lot of the management and inject new blood into our government. Accomplishing this is not easy because, effectively, there's no opposition in this country at all. Look at the referendum on the Lisbon Treaty; every major party supported it without equivocation. But you can take it from me, having read the document, that there was never a better case for opposition in and out of government. Instead, not only was there total consensus, but that consensus was completely uninformed. It is truly shocking that our political leaders presented themselves to the Irish people and said, "This is a good thing, but I haven't read it".

The Irish public and Irish business need much better governance at home and in Europe. In the European Parliament, our MEPs used to have a reputation for being drunk, for showing up late to meetings, for not showing up at all and for drinking in the morning. That situation has greatly improved, but we still are overdue a big shake-up at home. Many factors, external and personal, can contribute to creating a great entrepreneur. A business education is no burden to carry, but it is certainly not essential. When I'm hiring someone, I don't particularly look for an academic background. It is a filter system, but it is not the only one, and I've met some Harvard MBAs I wouldn't hire in a lifetime. I didn't go to college, so I can't give a fair critique of what it offers, but I would question the extent to which entrepreneurship can be taught. It is like music. You can teach someone how to play the guitar, but can you teach someone to play like Eric Clapton? I don't think so. Similarly, some people are more talented in the area of entrepreneurship than others.

People who are going to be successful as entrepreneurs will have a track record of risk-taking and they will have hunger, enthusiasm, raw intelligence, willingness to learn and street-smarts. I would always value people who have made mistakes, understood how they have made them and have learned from them. It generally takes me about an hour or two to recognise such a person. While formal education is not necessarily a great predictor of success, self-education throughout life is hugely important. Nobody can learn everything by themselves, and lessons can be found in many areas. In business, one can learn a lot from studying history, and looking at the lessons of history and reading history is the sort of thing that anybody can do for themselves. What matters is reading extensively and getting a broad view, from ancient, pre-Christian history right through to modern times. Study in this area is hugely enlightening, when it comes to knowing how we got to where we are. It is all in there: human nature, business, environment, trade, politics, conflict, innovation, disaster and everything else. Studying history is mind-expanding, so a good reading list is a useful tool for any successful entrepreneur.

One of the main reasons why I got involved in Libertas and the campaign for a 'No' vote in the Lisbon referendum was, as a businessman, looking into what the Lisbon treaty would mean for business. To start with, I read the draft of the European constitution. I was already involved in Eastern Europe, and I was looking into the potential benefits of accession. As someone who has had an interest in reading history for many years, I knew the massive impact that constitutions can have on business. I've already mentioned how the spirit of innovation and entrepreneurship flourishes in America. The reason why springs, ultimately, from the American constitution, because it gave people the breathing space that allowed innovation and invention and all the things that America has done for the world.

Then, look at what the Russian Revolution and that flawed formula did for Russia and the world in a hugely negative sense. As an enthusiastic European who has benefitted from doing business in Europe, I had hoped that the new constitution would give me new opportunities. I had already picked up 10 licenses in Europe, so who is going to be more pro-European integration than me?

I was not encouraged by what I read in that constitution, subsequently relabelled the Lisbon Treaty. In fact, it was a huge step backwards, for freedom, for business and for Europe generally. Some parts were good, but others were really very bad, and the biggest problem of all was that it would eliminate democratic accountability to the extent that it exists at all in any Brussels institutions that exercise real power. We should all remember that, without democracy, power is something that is much easier to give away than it is to wrest back. If passed, the Lisbon Treaty would have represented a shocking power grab, and created an environment that would have been total anathema to growth business and innovation across Europe.

What we need for Ireland, for Europe and for business is freedom, because without freedom there is no space for economic growth; there is only oligarchy. One of the most valuable lessons to learn from history is that men's greed for power without accountability is endless and, as Thomas Jefferson said, the price of freedom is eternal vigilance. If the alternate future envisioned by the Lisbon Treaty were to come into being, we would only see enterprises with no more than a passing resemblance to what we think of as business, rather like what we see in Russia. Business would exist at the whim of a political elite, which would decide whether or not an enterprise survives. Entrepreneurs would be forced to become courtiers; they would be turned into 'grantrapreneurs'. They would become people who depend for their business and their livelihoods on grants, subsidies, hand-outs and special favours. As a new business, trying to get in on any of the European Union's so-called 'framework plans', for this, that and the other is almost impossible. Instead, these programmes function as a way of funnelling tax-payers' money to subsidise inefficient industries that just cannot compete in the global marketplace. Right across Europe, we are all taxed far too much, directly and indirectly, and given sub-standard services in return. We have a system where risk and innovation, the foundations of successful entrepreneurship, are actively discouraged, and people made increasingly dependent on the State. In these situations, societies lose confidence in themselves and lose hope for the future. This is not a theory; it is something that is already happening all over Europe, and we see it in the fact that the European population is plummeting.

Having children is the ultimate statement of a civilisation's confidence in itself and the best investment humanity can make in itself is future generations. Current figures suggest that, in 40 or 50 years, there will be about 140 million fewer Europeans than there are today, which is a situation equivalent to the disappearance of two major countries! This is the defining challenge of our times, and it is the real question that faces Europe.

> *The Europe that we should all want to be part of*
> *will be one that embodies democratic accountability*
> *and embraces risk-taking and entrepreneurship,*
> *in the wider sense, and will be a place in which*
> *innovation and families both grow.*

At the moment, I am still very focused on innovation and entrepreneurship, and the most important issue from that point of view is making sure that the Europe in which we live and do business will be the right place for us. A properly democratic environment, championing the rule of law, is the essential foundation. This is why I founded Libertas, to take the issues facing Europe to the people of Europe, who all deserve to answer the question: "Do you want the kind of Europe as outlined in the Lisbon Treaty, which is not going to get us anywhere, and hands over power to an elite that is unlikely ever to hand it back to you, or do you want a Europe that's democratic and accountable, transparent in the way it operates and can chart a course for a future that everybody can get excited about?".

This is one situation in which we are faced with a need whose time has come, but about which people haven't thought very much. I suspect that, in retrospect, it is going to be like the invention of the wheel. Someone had to do it first, and then it was obvious, and everyone must have asked themselves, "Why didn't *we* do that?".

At the moment, more than 80% of our laws are now originating from Brussels, but we don't have the tools to be able to democratically monitor and control Brussels yet. Whether Libertas provides those tools or not remains to be seen. The fact is that few events occur that can form or catalyse the changes that we need. The European elections are an ideal opportunity, but they are not there every year. We could wait until the next round, but a lot of damage could have been done by then, considering the trends in the world today. A lot can happen in a few years. Again, to look at the lessons of history, we can consider the transition from Weimar Germany to the Third Reich. In a very concentrated period of time, there was Germany's occupation of the Rhineland and invasion of the Sudetenland, the annexation of Austria. All of those things happened in a very concentrated period of time. Hitler could easily have been stopped when his armies occupied the Rhineland but, by the time they got into Sudetenland, it was already too late and war was inevitable.

We need to be able to act before that sort of situation is reached at all. There is no pan-European politic, and we need one, so the questions that we face – and they are real, serious, business questions – are: Can Libertas identify and carefully scrutinise enough candidates of very high calibre to be able to take a significant number of seats in the European Parliament to be effective? Can it raise the money to fund that campaign? The answer to those two questions right now is "possibly".

If I become satisfied that it can, we will need to spend many tens of millions of Euro to run that campaign across 27 Member States of the European Union, and field a large number of candidates, all of whom have to be excellent, and have to be people who didn't want to be politicians as their first choice. They will have to be aggressively canvassed, so that they can be persuaded to leave their university chairs or private sector jobs, or the public sector, to give five years of their lives to something that is hugely serious; putting this continent and the world on course to head in the right direction. We would have to be extraordinarily careful, making sure that values and objectives are shared, as the organisation is built across multiple Member States of the European Union. There is safety in numbers, so when there's a critical mass, what Libertas might work to achieve will have become the obvious thing to do. So far, I have been pleasantly surprised by the number of people who are prepared to take the risk. At the moment, it is astonishing how many senior politicians across Europe recognise that Lisbon is a bad deal, but don't want to stand alone. The Irish people have said, "The emperor has no clothes", but our political class hasn't got the courage or the entrepreneurship or the intelligence of the Irish people and we have our ministers apologising for us and saying that we have to figure out what's wrong in Ireland. They have drunk the Kool-Aid from Brussels, but the Irish people did not.

The Irish took a risk and made the right decision, not just for themselves but for almost half a billion people across Europe and that – embracing risk-taking, being involved in innovation – is ultimately what entrepreneurship is all about.

> *We have a whole generation of young and youngish*
> *entrepreneurs, who are out there doing remarkable things.*
> *They provide a sharp contrast to our political class,*
> *which remains firmly in the old school of thinking,*
> *looking askance on risk-taking, entrepreneurship*
> *and out-of-the-box thinking.*

6
LIAM GRIFFIN

Liam Griffin, one of Ireland's leading entrepreneurs and hoteliers, owns the Monart Destination Spa, Ferrycarrig Hotel and Hotel Kilkenny. The Monart Destination Spa has been rated by *Forbes* magazine as one of the World's Top 10 Super Spas.

Liam is also deeply involved in the GAA, having managed the Wexford team to All-Ireland hurling success in 1996. He contributes as a sports columnist and commentator to *The Sunday Tribune* and on radio.

A SCÉIL FHÉIN

I grew up in Rosslare Strand, in Co. Wexford, the son of a Clare Guard and a Wexford woman. My mother was originally from Ballygarrett in North Wexford, and my parents met when my father was stationed close by. My mother and grandmother must have been among the very first people in Ireland to run a farm guesthouse. My grandfather had died when my mother was only 12, leaving my grandmother with four children in a very difficult economic climate. As her house was close to Courtown, she started to take in paying guests, which was how the family started in the hotel business. We have now had four generations of the same family in business.

My first contact with a real business person was actually with my mother. She worked in the hospitality business until she was in her mid-80s. In the beginning, she had guests in our house in Rosslare, and then my father built a chalet beside the house. At the same time, my parents ran a knitwear business in the winter which, being religious, they named 'Marie Theresa Knitwear'. My mother was the best marketer in the world. She got on her bicycle, and went into Wexford, where she secured a contract to make the uniforms for all the local schools. She got the contract for the de la Salle in Waterford, as well, which is where my brothers and I went to school. When my father retired early from the Guards, my parents sold off their knitwear business and put a deposit on a small, run-down hotel in Rosslare Harbour. My first job in the hotel business was helping my father to put slates on the roof of it because it was leaking. From the age of 12 or so, I used to help out in all sorts of ways.

I boarded at school. I had been dreading it, but I loved it, especially because I was good at hurling and football, and played on the team for the school. In fact, I captained the first ever de la Salle team to a reach a Harty Cup hurling final. I'm still very grateful to the de la Salle brothers for all they did for me.

I would have loved to have become a professional sportsman, but there just weren't any professional opportunities in Irish sports at the time. Instead, feeling very loyal to my parents, I decided to go to the Shannon College of Hotel Management when I left secondary school in the mid 1960s. The director of the college was Jorgen Blum, a Swiss gentleman, who ran it like a barracks. This was the era of the Beatles, yet we had to have our hair cut short, and our nails and attire were inspected every day. In retrospect, I can see that the discipline was fantastic. Presentation is obviously a hugely important aspect of working in the hotel industry. The training we received was great, and we had a lot of wonderful experiences including, at the age of 19, being taken on a wine tour of France, Germany and Switzerland. I also remember very vividly being taken to Verdun, to the site where the bones of the dead from the First World War were kept. Years later, I took my own family.

We've got to facilitate people starting in business, because 75% of all businesses in this country are family-run.

I stayed in Shannon for two years, getting a grounding in the business and playing on the Clare team, which was wonderful for my father, a Clare man, because it meant that I was now associated in his mind with the greats of the Clare GAA scene. After two years, I went to Switzerland to acquire work experience with the Movenpick Corporation in Zurich. The business had been started by a Mr Prager, who initially had just one small café in Zurich, and then extended the model. His system was a forerunner of the McDonald's corporation later on, albeit serving a more upscale segment of the market. After that, I worked in Llangollen in North Wales in a Trust House Forte hotel, called the Royal Hotel. After another year, I returned to Shannon to present my thesis and graduated. I had a very clear idea of what I wanted to achieve, and how I would achieve it. I had already experienced an excellent Swiss operation, and one of the world's best hotel organisations, so I felt that the next step would be to work with an American company, so I arranged to attend an interview for a job with the Intercontinental Hotel in Dublin. When I arrived, there seemed to be at least 20 people waiting to be interviewed and I realised that I would have to do something to stand out from the crowd. So, when the interviewer asked, "Why should I hire you?", I said, "Because I'm cheap. I'll work for free". I offered to work for free for a month on condition that, if they liked the way I worked, I would be kept on and compensated retrospectively. They accepted this, and I stayed for three years, during which period I was promoted several times.

By then, I was really looking forward to moving back to Rosslare, but I felt that it would be useful to join the Irish Tourism Board, if I could, because I wanted to get a look at global tourism and how Irish tourism related to the tourism industry worldwide. I was sure that this would be a really good way to round off my experience before going home.

By now, my father had died, and my mother was running the business on her own. She was well able to do it, but I did feel eager to return. I had had a wonderful childhood and felt strongly rooted in Wexford. My CV was good, so I was accepted by Bord Fáilte, where I worked as a standards advisor for a few years, before taking over the family business in 1974. As I had hoped, this was a great learning experience.

The culture of the hospitality industry in Ireland has changed utterly in the course of the last few decades. Before, hotels had rickety stairs, rooms with no bathrooms and bedrooms so small you couldn't swing a kitten in them, let alone a cat. As Ireland began the process of modernising, models for the hotel business came in from abroad, such as the Intercontinental and Trust House Forte hotels. Now, I feel we might be in danger of swinging too far in the direction of corporate anonymity. It is hard for a hotel to retain charm when it is huge, and there does seem to be a bit of a backlash at present, with small hotels being developed again. In our business, we have always tried to maintain the best of international standards, while maintaining a personal touch. One of the great things about the hotel business is the fact that the person who has education, experience and what I call the 'fire in their belly' can make it all the way to the top very quickly. That's just one of the things that makes the hotel industry so fantastic, but there's lots more. I love my business. In what other job could I look at wine, get involved with architecture, design menus and work with interior decoration, all at the same time?

I feel I've so many opportunities for creative expression in
my own business that it's fantastic.

I'm glad to say that I haven't made too many mistakes in business. The fact is that people who have lots of money can afford to make mistakes; I've spent my working life on the margins to keep business going. We have taken some gambles. For instance, when we bought a hotel in Kilkenny, it was a big gamble, but the location was fantastic and it worked out well. Similarly, in Wexford, there was a lot of agonising before we bought the Ferrycarrig Hotel. We sold the old family hotel in Rosslare, because we had outgrown it. It was a heart-wrenching business, but there's no room for being too sentimental in business; you have to make sound decisions. More recently, we developed a destination spa in Monart, near Enniscorthy.

Marketing ... the biggest problem in every business at the moment is sales but, once you have sales, you can get all the other things.

I think that the Irish make fantastic businesspeople, and I particularly admire the self-employed. These are people who perhaps could have looked at the option of getting an easy job in the public service that would offer them a huge amount of time off, and have chosen to take on the stress of running their own business, with the long hours and the risk and also the excitement. These are people who want to go out there and do their own thing. In Ireland, 75% of businesses are family-owned, which means that there's a huge army of entrepreneurs quietly working all hours in every day. To speak for myself, I am perfectly happy to work long hours, often seven days a week, in the knowledge that I've never been a burden on the State. People who are not self-employed often assume that anyone who owns their own business is hugely wealthy, but the fact is that there are thousands upon thousands of small business owners working long hours around the year for modest returns and these are the people who do the most for the Irish economy.

One of the big problems facing young people starting out in business today is the fact that we have created a culture that places way too much emphasis on work-life balance or, to be more accurate, on the idea that one doesn't have to work hard. Of course, it is important to have some leisure time, but we need to teach young people that work is important. Apart from anything else, most of us get more satisfaction at work than in any other way. We have to eliminate the notion that work is something that just has to be done. It's not a notion prevalent around the world. For me, work is a great place to be! It's just like playing a match. When two teams are pitched against each other, and there's the knowledge that your team can win if you just put in the effort, it will happen. Hesitation is fatal.

In my business in particular, I would be afraid that potential business leaders of the future would be put off starting their careers in a hotel because we have taught them to expect a working life in which they'll never have to work weekends or evenings or make a huge effort. This, unfortunately, is a message that they are receiving very strongly from our Government in the form of its services. The Irish State has allowed the notion to develop over the years that the world starts on Monday at 9am and finishes at 5pm on a Friday. We have social and health services that expect people to have crises only during office hours. This culture is very damaging to the future business prospects of a new generation and, if we would like to maintain and grow a modern economy, it is crucial that we eliminate it. The whole notion of days when the entire nation is off-work dates to before the Industrial Revolution, when shift work was introduced; that's how out of date it is!

Many of the real heroes of Irish business are not loudly trumpeted at all as they go about their work, quietly creating jobs and prosperity for Ireland. We hear about it when a foreign company comes to Ireland and opens up a business, but when an Irish business creates jobs, it doesn't even make the local papers. Again, we have a problem with Government in this respect. Their PR machine ensures that when a foreign company is attracted to Ireland, the media is all over the story. At the same time, the Irish Government has failed to offer real leadership; it's all about consensus now, and that's certainly a good thing, but there are times when we need leadership and management, and for somebody to just take charge and be the boss. That is true for sports, and it is true for business. I sincerely hope that we are now entering a new era where people say, "We're listening to you. We hear you. But this is now how we're going to do it. It's fair, we've taken your ideas on board, but we're going to do it this way". Without leadership, we don't have accountability and we will never have effective public services helping businesses to grow and to continue to employ people. Of course, there are some fantastic people in public service, but at the end of the day they must deliver a service; that's their job.

Personally, I think that we have conceded far too much power. Another challenge facing people starting out in business, or indeed continuing to run businesses, is the fact that the Government appears to have abdicated responsibility for the way rates and taxes are levied. Now, local authorities can levy huge charges without warning, challenging the viability of what would otherwise be thriving enterprises. There are scores of stealth taxes on businesses today, and no way to demand accountability from authorities. A local shop overcharging for bread can be reported to the National Consumer Agency, but government authorities are not answerable to the very people who pay them. This is a huge challenge to entrepreneurship, which is not fully understood. Instead of punishing people for starting out in business, we should facilitate them. Why are Irish businesses paying so much more for basic utilities than our neighbours in Europe and the UK? The answer is obvious. Irish businesspeople are here for the long haul, and I don't see why Irish businesses should be punished for existing, while so much help and assistance goes to foreign multinationals, which could leave at any moment.

> *Attitude is more important than education in the workplace. Attitude is important because, after you get the right attitude, you can get everything.*

Nothing can beat experience but, of course, education and training are important. Anyone starting a business has to have an idea that will work; they have to be sensible about it, and work out all the facts and figures; and then find a way to work hard and really enjoy their work, because the person who enjoys their work will never find it burdensome. Formal education can be helpful, but continuous learning is essential. In my case, I had never wanted to read a book at all until I went to Shannon, when I took a keen interest.

Whatever field one is in, it is very important to know what is going on in the world, and to read serious writing relating to one's industry, as well as making contacts and speaking with people who are in the business. In our hotel group, we have continuous learning for all the employees at the craft level, and frequent meetings where we discuss ideas and things that we've read that are relevant to the business. We bring in trainers periodically, and our Human Resources department offers specific training too.

The people who I admire are those who are outspoken, who say what they really believe, and who don't shilly-shally.

Despite the commitments of business, I have remained deeply passionate about sport. I have spent a lot of my life – from 1981 to 2006 – coaching teams. This often meant working until two in the morning, and then being out on the pitch early the next day, or finishing work at 6.30pm, going training and then returning to work. When I managed the Wexford team in the 1990s, I used to get up at 5am on occasions to figure out my plans for the day, both for the business and for the team. I never found it a burden, and I never took time off work.

It's all about attitude. Attitude is everything. Attitude brings discipline. We see this in sports all the time. You might have the best team in Ireland but, without investing in them from a psychological point of view, they are not going to win. It's the same at work. When interviewing people for a job, I feel that a lot should be about gut instinct. It's not all about the CV; if you feel instinctively that this is a person with the right attitude, you are probably correct.

The issue of attitude is closely aligned to the whole issue of emotional intelligence, or what is referred to as 'EQ' – emotional quotient. Emotional intelligence has a huge correlation with what we refer to as being 'street-smart'. A person who may not necessarily have a great academic background can bring a lot of emotional intelligence to work, which is something that is enormously important in a service industry like ours.

All entrepreneurs will learn quickly that the most important aspect of any business is marketing and sales, and also that marketing is a huge expense for any business. In our organisation, we do a lot of guest questionnaires and we do a lot of feedback from our clientele, so we build up databases, which makes it possible to keep in touch with former clients and send them news about special offers and so on. It is very important for us to maintain a good website, and keep it optimised, whereas the correlation between money spent on newspaper advertising and sales is much less clear.

In general, I believe that Irish people are quite good at marketing, and that they have improved hugely in this area in the course of the last 10 years. However, Irish business people will have to contend with the undeniable fact that there are too many shops and business in most areas at the current time. In my industry, for example, the Government gives permission for hotel after hotel after hotel, despite the fact that they are shutting people out of business. Their interest in allowing new businesses in whatever sector to open, even when there is a demonstrable lack of need, is the fact that new businesses generate more rates. We all need to work at creating an environment in which indigenous businesses are not punished for existing, but helped to flourish, because these are the organisations that are in it for the long haul; international companies are much more likely to leave when there are better opportunities elsewhere.

Of course, the hours can be long and awkward in the hotel industry but, speaking personally, I didn't want to work anywhere else. One of the most important elements in a happy life is the opportunity for creative expression, and my industry offers this possibility every day.

So the guy said to me – he was probably sick of listening to everybody else talking – "Why should I hire you?", and I said, "Because I'm cheap. I'll work for free!"

7
ANNE HERATY

Anne Heraty founded CPL in Dublin in 1989. CPL is a leading Irish provider of recruitment and human resource services across a broad industry skill-base. Its services include specialist recruitment; work force management; payroll and outsourcing services. CPL clients include world-leading companies, public and private institutions and small and medium size enterprises.

The company operates through a number of quality brands such as *Careers Register* – finance and accounting; *Medical Recruitment Specialists* – healthcare; *Techskills* – engineering; *Thornshaw* and *CPL Science* – pharmaceutical and scientific; *Ann O'Brien* – office; *Multiflex* – light industrial; *BroadReach* – executive search; and *CPL Managed Services* – human resource and workforce management.

CPL employs an internal workforce of 250 employees and offers long and short-term work to over 15,000 people each year. Operating through a network of 12 offices including Ireland, UK and Poland, CPL offers career opportunities through all stages of an individual's career in permanent, contract and temporary positions.

Anne Heraty was winner of the *Ernst & Young Entrepreneur of the Year* award in 2006.

A SCÉIL FHÉIN

I grew up in a village in North Longford called Ballinalee, where my parents ran a farm, a shop and a pub. My father was also the local undertaker—it was the usual family business in the country. I went to national school in the village, and then I went to secondary school in Newtown Forbes, which is also in County Longford. My father died when I was 16 and, from that period on, my mother ran the family business on her own, with everyone in the family pitching in to help. My mother was really very passionate about her business. She used to tell us children that we should get good, secure, pensionable jobs, but the fact is that children learn from seeing what their parents do, not from listening to what they say, and what we saw every day was a woman who was driven, excited and passionate about her business, with an incredible work ethic. My mother was the closest I had to a role model in my early years in business.

After finishing secondary school, I went to University College Dublin, where I did a BA in maths and economics through the Faculty of Arts. While there's no direct link between my educational background and my professional field, I feel that education is hugely important for anyone going into business, and know that it has been a great help to me. I graduated from university in 1984, into a very bleak economic and cultural environment in which unemployment was 17% or 18%, and most young people were emigrating because there just didn't seem to be much of a future in Ireland.

I would actively encourage people to start their own business.

Since I graduated from University College Dublin in 1984, the business culture in Ireland has changed hugely. Despite ups and downs, the culture is much more optimistic and positive. In the 1980s, it seemed inevitable that the brightest young people would emigrate, and there was very little entrepreneurship and very little sense of hope of success and achievement. Things are utterly different today.

My first proper job was in 1986 as a sales executive with Xerox. Xerox offered excellent training, and I learned a great deal, especially about how to sell professionally. I worked in a number of other sales positions, and then I registered with an employment agency, looking for a new opportunity. As it happened, the agency asked me if I would be interested in working in recruitment with them and offered me training in the field. I thought about it and decided to do exactly that. I loved recruitment from the outset, and had found the work that I was born to do.

After a year and a half, I decided to set up my own business, and was fortunate to get financial backing, direction and support from Keith O'Malley, who was the founder of the Professional Placement Group. I started in a tiny office in College Green, with literally just a desk, a phone and a copy of the *Golden Pages*. The reason why I wanted to set up my own business in recruitment was because I felt passionately that one's career is right up there with one's health, wealth and happiness. Recruitment companies at that time in Ireland were generalist; I could be recruiting an accountant today, a programmer tomorrow, and maybe a sales guy the next day. I felt that, if I was to become a trusted advisor to someone about something as important as their career, I really needed to have a depth of knowledge about the sector in which they worked and the opportunities available for them to progress.

In recruitment, I found a field that really suited my skills completely. I loved working in that area, and I still do. I very much enjoy working with people, and I haven't wavered in my belief that a good job and a rewarding career are fundamental to happiness. Just think of how much time we spend in the workplace; a career can provide both something to do and something to look forward to and I see working with people about something so very important as a privilege.

In the early days of working in my own business, I made lots of mistakes – and I continue to make them to the present – but I don't dwell on them or let them define me. With respect to mistakes made in business, my only advice is that you've just got to learn from them and move on quickly. Anyone who wants to run their own business has to get comfortable with the reality that they are going to make mistakes and even, at times, to experience failure. I learn as much from failure as success. Business people should not be defined by their mistakes; it takes great courage to start over and I admire anyone who does.

To succeed, I would say, "Hire the right people".
No other thing. Because, you know ... talented people are
what drive growth in businesses.

Throughout the 1990s, CPL focused on the information technology sector. We built our business placing people in permanent and contract IT solutions. In 1999, we took the company public, with the intention of building a number of specialist recruitment businesses. Today, we operate in the ICT, healthcare, pharma, accounting and finance, sales, human resources, office administration and light industrial sectors. Each business has a strong specialist ethos and operates quite independently within the umbrella of the organisation. Over the group as a whole, we have between 1,800 customers a year, encompassing everything from hospitals in the public sector to multinationals to small businesses. The people they are looking for are similarly diverse. The businesses are all substantial in their own right. The healthcare division, for example, has a turnover of about €30 million.

Until relatively recently, we worked only in Ireland, and we have often been asked how we managed to work in such a small labour market and remain specialist, but the fact is that anybody who is looking for a career move needs to know that they are dealing with a recruiter who really understands their sector. Generally, the way we work is that a client will come to us with a specific requirement, and we will go out and do a thorough search of the marketplace to find people with those particular skills. Because of all the resources available to us, including our database and our deep network of contacts, we really understand the capabilities of the people whom we put forward for positions. The labour market today is truly global so, in CPL, we don't just look in Ireland to find people with the skills we need, but across in the world in that particular sector.

My work is challenging and always interesting, in good times and bad. For instance, when we went public in 1999, 95% of our revenue came from the IT sector. When there was a global downturn in 2001 as a result of the dotcoms bust and the fallout after September 11th, CPL went through a very tough period. The most important lesson I learned was that it doesn't matter how difficult the economic environment is, the crucial thing is the quality of the people on your team, people with the will and attitude to succeed. Many of the people who are now in key management positions at CPL came through that period very well, with a combination of positive attitude and hard work. In difficult times, it is very important to understand one's strengths and capabilities. Speaking personally, I knew that I certainly didn't have all the answers on my own, and we worked as a team and found a path forward and new opportunities for growth. It was during this time that the foundation stones for our current expansion were laid. We stayed focussed and built our market share by really staying close to our customers.

While every organisation is different, some things are the same in all businesses. These are attitude, ethics and knowledge of one's own field. In CPL, for example, we have recruiters who really know and understand the areas they work in. In the field of healthcare, some of our recruiters are former nurses. That means that they completely understand their area, and know who to look for, and how a medical career should build and develop. Across sectors, one of the things that strikes me the most is the fact that industry is changing very quickly, and careers are changing at a similar place. In recruitment, it's essential to keep up with that speed of change, and understand it very well.

You have choices in life and you make those choices so ...
it's about work choice rather than work-life balance.
It's a subtle difference, but it's an important difference.

There are many people to admire in Irish business today. I have huge respect for people who have built businesses, either as entrepreneurs or as professional managers. As well as the big names in business, I feel that there are thousands of unsung heroes who have done truly exceptional things, but about whom nobody hears very much. In terms of the wonderful transformation of the Irish economy, the highly-skilled managers in some of the multinationals have worked, very quietly and hard, to bring jobs to Ireland. As I understand it, they have to compete with all the other subsidiaries in their organisation around the globe to ensure that their branch wins. They have had to fight extremely hard to win jobs for Ireland and, in my view, they do not get enough recognition for what they have done in terms of the growth of the Irish economy.

The business culture in Ireland has changed hugely since I graduated in 1984. Notwithstanding what is happening at the moment, it is much more optimistic and much more positive.

T he whole issue of balancing life and work is much debated; I think of it as a work-life choice rather than a work-life balance and I am lucky to be able to make that choice. Of course, I relax outside business, but the simple fact is that I love what I do, and I honestly feel that this is what I was born to do. In fact, I can't imagine doing anything else, and when people ask me why I am still working in the same field, the simple answer is that this is what I love doing. After all, what is the one thing that really makes a difference to a business? Hiring the right people! Sometimes, I feel a bit frustrated, because I think that many people actually don't fully understand this. Hiring the right people is what transforms businesses and drives shareholder value. I look forward to the day when we can account accurately for the impact of hiring the right people. The difference between hiring a top performer and hiring an average performer can be as high as four-to-one in our business. Knowing that, thinking about it and wondering how we can continue to perform better and better is the sort of thing that exercises my mind all the time.

I think it's a positive thing for universities to have a chair of entrepreneurship, provided the entrepreneurship chair is held by somebody who has set up a business or who has that mindset.

Within CPL, we have excellent interaction as a team, and we learn a lot from each other. Learning within our organisation is really very important; we have an extensive training programme in place to develop our people. Training has an immense impact on people's ability, so we provide a great deal of formal training; some of our people are with the National College of Ireland, studying management development, and we also use SkillNets. As well as learning in the context of attending formal training, we all can learn a huge amount from our colleagues, too. One of the reasons why people decide to change jobs is that they reach a point where they are no longer learning from their boss or peer group. In today's workplace, things are changing so fast, that there's no choice but to learn. We've got to run to keep up! Anybody who would like to start their own business should invest in their education and skills. In today's environment, our ability and attitude to learning can be more important than the particular skill or qualification we have. Skills can be acquired, if we have the capacity of interest in learning. My advice to business people is that they should hire for attitude every time, and train for skill.

Of the various achievements that we've had at CPL, I think the best has been our team-building. We have a core group of people who have been working here for a long time, and we have added a lot to that group in the last four or five years. When I find somebody whom I know to be really talented, it is a bit like winning the Lotto! There's nothing like seeing someone's capability and knowing that they will have a dramatic impact.

Now that CPL is expanding internationally, the key to our success will be the people we hire to drive the business. It's a question of getting the right person for the right position and matching their skills with what they need to do. I feel that the time has come for CPL to make our mark internationally, as other companies like the Kerry Group or CRH have done. Maybe that sounds ambitious, but that's my vision and that is what I am working towards. We already have very successful offices in Prague, Bratislava, Brno, Warsaw and Barcelona. In recent years, many people have come to work in Ireland, and this has been a wonderful opportunity for CPL; we have about 50 nationalities working with us in the CPL Group. This means that, as we open our offices overseas, we are able to have them led by people who already integral members of the CPL team. Because our approach is very much about putting people first, we are setting up in countries where we already have the people with the capacity to grow a business. Our manager in Poland worked with us here in Ireland in international recruitment, for example. These are people who really understand our culture in CPL, and who know how we think and work. They have built trust in the company, and we have built trust in them. We do not micro-manage them, because they are talented people who have a vision.

I have a very simple philosophy. In order to have a good, successful and happy life, there's probably only three things you really need: someone to love, something to do, and something to look forward to.

I won the *Ernst & Young Entrepreneur of the Year* award in 2006, and it was a truly wonderful experience. Initially, I didn't know what I was getting into, but now I can safely say that what Enda Kelly and Ernst & Young are doing for entrepreneurship in Ireland today is just phenomenal. The *Entrepreneur of the Year* programme is really driving change on the ground with respect to how people think about entrepreneurship and everything associated with it. As a result of my involvement with the programme, I met some very talented individuals. Running one's own business is so absorbing, and involves being so very focussed that it can be difficult to connect with other people who are doing similar things, unless they just happen to be friends. In the programme, I met lots of Irish entrepreneurs who have set up marvellous businesses that, otherwise, I wouldn't have been aware of, and I realised that we are all facing similar challenges and issues. I learned a lot about what is actually happening on the ground in Ireland. In recent years, I feel that entrepreneurship has begun to be viewed much more favourably by the Irish people in general, and Enda Kelly has certainly contributed enormously to this.

In today's environment, you need to be IT-literate and to
have certain capability around certain skills. But, once that's
a given, it's your attitude that determines your success.

I n Ireland, we could have a stronger focus on entrepreneurship in
our universities. By providing people studying technical
disciplines, such as engineering or the sciences, with business
skills, it is likely that we would have more business start-ups in those
sectors. Many of these students are Ireland's future businesspeople,
the brightest minds of their generation, and many of them will be the
best and brightest entrepreneurs. I would be in favour of the notion
that universities establish Chairs of Entrepreneurship, with the proviso
that these be held by people who have actually set up businesses.
There are already some examples: Sam McCauley, who established
McCauley Pharmacies, among other things, is the Chair in the
Waterford Institute of Technology. In general, we have a lot to do in
the area of linking business with academia. There is also a lot to be
done in the field of sales and marketing, especially with respect to the
international market. We pride ourselves on being a trading nation,
and it is true that more Irish companies are starting to sell
internationally, but it has to be said that more needs to be done to
develop selling skills internationally. Clearly, the potential is there.
Multinational organisations have been hugely successful in terms of
using Ireland as a launch pad into Europe. There are so many benefits:
we're English-speaking; we are on the periphery; and we're good
European citizens. We have had a great run in Ireland, and have been
very successful at attracting foreign investment. Now, it's our turn. We
have to start looking outward and begin building the international
capacity of indigenous industries.

I would say to anyone looking to start their own business,
"Invest in your education – and then in your skills".

T his is a wonderful time for young people in Ireland who are planning to start their own businesses, and this is something that I would actively encourage them to do. Of course, the economy is now growing at a slower rate than over the course of the last 10 years, but this is not really the issue. Ireland remains a good place to do business, and there are many opportunities for those who have ideas, and who feel passionate and committed about them. I think that one of the most important things that would-be entrepreneurs must understand is that their commitment to their business must be complete and absolute. They will have to understand the nature of success and failure, because they will invariably experience both, and they will have to be able to deal with both.

When you're starting a business, you've got to understand
the completeness of the commitment.

8

MICHAEL HERBERT

Michael Herbert is now chairman of the board of the Windsor Motor Group. As chief executive officer, he oversaw the group's phenomenal growth and expansion in Ireland. He has worked for the Windsor Group for some 15 years and is a past president of the Society of the Irish Motor Industry.

Windsor Motor Group was established in 1968 and, since then, has grown to be Ireland's largest dealer group. It is best known for its strong relationship with Nissan, as it operates nine Nissan dealerships in Airside, Belgard, Bray, Cork, Deansgrange, Galway, Liffey Valley, Raheny and Rialto. In addition, it also operates four Chevrolet and SsangYong dealerships at Bray, Deansgrange, Cork and Galway and two Opel dealerships in Liffey Valley and Airside Motor Park. It has a turnover of €270m and 450 staff.

A SCÉIL FHÉIN

Born in Birmingham of Irish parents in the early 1950s, I still have very fond memories of my former years in England. Ironically, a number of my earlier school teachers were Irish, which must have given me an early taste of what it would be like to live in Ireland.

As a family of five, we travelled to Ireland on holidays each year to Arklow, which was a real treat. In those times, it seemed like a long way to go!

We moved to Ireland in the mid-1960s. It was a big 'culture shock', coming from inner city Birmingham to a suburb of Dublin. It felt like a move to the countryside at the time, having lived in the city for so long.

My father was a secondary school teacher and my mother a shopkeeper. Despite my father's work-role, he rarely became involved in my schooling and very much left me to my own devices; in some ways, this was good as I had to take responsibility for myself and my education.

The initial taste of going to school in inner city Dublin, Strand Street, to the 'Christian Brothers' was interesting and impacted on me quite strongly. My view of the clergy was that they were upright, fair and led by example; however, the level of corporal punishment from canes to leathers was shocking in the extreme, very brutal and totally unnecessary.

If there is one thing that stands out from this period, it is the reaction of inner city Dublin boys to my English (Brummie) accent; it didn't take too long for them to 'convert' me to speak Dublinese – which included a few words not found in the Oxford dictionary.

As a student, I worked hard but I would hardly say I enjoyed the atmosphere at school (and not just at Strand Street). Looking back, I see that a lot of teachers taught by using 'fear' as their key teaching tool – "Learn this or else!" – lots of stick and very little carrot. At that time, college was not high on the agenda after the Leaving Certificate for most students and it certainly wasn't for me. I couldn't wait to move on to the next stage and start earning money.

Did I know what the next stage was? No ... and it took a while for me to discover what I wanted to do.

*Ireland is a superb place for entrepreneurship, despite the
fact that the media is always harping on the negatives.
There's so much being achieved!*

D uring my years in secondary school, my mother ran a hardware shop in Palmerstown and, later, a grocery shop in Lucan. The experiences I gained from working in both of these outside of school time was to prove influential and indeed invaluable in my future, despite the fact that I did not recognise or appreciate this at the time.

I will give you a few examples of these experiences. The hardware business was difficult to make money from because of the fluctuation in sales, mainly caused by strikes in big organisations like CIE (buses and trains), Guinness Brewery, the building industry and so on.

Once, there was a strike going on – there were lots of them at that time – and business dropped like a stone. A lack of confidence seemed to come over everyone.

To counteract this and to develop the business, my mother was inclined to promise a lot ... and deliver more. As soon as I would get in the door from school, I would be on my bike delivering dustbins, kitchen cabinets, planks of wood and lots of other bulky items. As not many people had a second car, delivery was a great bonus for them. I often had to fit the delivered items and soon became very adept at balancing on a kitchen chair while drilling holes in walls to fit presses, mirrors and other such items.

What I realise now in retrospect is how my mother was building her reputation for excellent customer service, whilst at the same time she kept me busy learning some practical skills – which no doubt aided in keeping me out of trouble.

After many strikes, my parents moved to Lucan and opened a grocery shop, the logic being that people must eat, even during a strike. This was high volume, low margin, fast-moving and profitable. If customer service was big in the hardware business, it was even bigger in grocery. One bad apple meant the whole order was wrong! So 99% wasn't good enough, it had to be 100%!

Taking orders by phone called for careful listening, accurate recording and then proper selection of goods to reach the 100% score. This was a real education for me and contributed greatly to my awareness of customer management. On top of this, I would deliver and, despite this being a very basic job, I learned how important it was 'to get the basics right'. Saying you would deliver at 3.00pm but arriving at either 2.30pm or 3.30pm was a disaster. Early meant the customer was doing something else which you interrupted and being late meant that you 'dropped the ball'. Punctuality was respected and admired, it put a smile on people's faces and generated repeat business, recommendations and, for me, sometimes a tip.

To me, this was more of a real education than I could have got from university. I never knew then how much these years of shop work would influence my thinking and my life in future careers and I certainly didn't appreciate or recognise any of the benefits at the time.

One benefit I did recognise was that I always got the use of the family car for Friday and Saturday nights. Even though it was only a Morris Minor, it was capable of carrying lots of my friends to far-away venues and adventures.

I love teamwork and working together.

So, when I had reached 17 and had completed my Leaving Certificate, I had to figure out my passion. What I knew was that it wasn't to run a grocery shop, despite my parent's best wishes. What I also knew, or should I say 'felt', was that I wanted to work with cars. Not that there was any history of cars in the family, my father was a Morris Minor driver only and my mother couldn't drive at all. My curiosity for cars led me to 'play' with components like carburettors, starter motors and dynamos, to take them apart and to re-assemble them, having found out how they worked. I had become an apprentice to a workshop manual.

I decided to follow my passion and go find a job in the motor industry. Leaving home one morning, I had no CV and was armed with nothing but my mouth to explain what I wanted and to 'sell myself' to some potential employer. At my third port of call, I struck gold and was interviewed by Sean Mooney, Service Manager of Hartigan's in Parkgate Street (now Gowans). Within five minutes, he recommended that, with Leaving Certificate qualifications, I could work in the service reception office in a position we refer to today as a 'Service Advisor'.

Well, this job was really 'up my alley', as it involved dealing with telephone customers who needed repairs / servicing and making arrangements to suit their needs. All my shop experience paid off and I settled into this role quickly. Customers were used to being treated in a 'less than exceptional' manner by the motor trade and I found that they really appreciated when they were handled with proper attention, had bills explained in detail, received good communication and had their car ready on time. Needless to say, I enjoyed every day, despite my small salary of £8 per week.

One big bonus was getting to drive some really exotic cars like Jaguar XJ6s and E-types, Rover V8s and MGBs. In fact, I was privileged to bring one home on the odd occasion, although I couldn't afford the petrol bill to go out driving it at night!

Within two years, Sean Mooney moved to a new company as Garage Group Manager. This was PMPA (now AXA), at the time Ireland's biggest car insurer, as well as a newly emerging garage group. Sean asked me to move with him, which I happily did, adopting a similar, but more senior, role with a better salary.

You become a team and all start pulling in the right direction.
Once that happens, you can go to the moon with a business.

Opportunity knocked for me to progress after another 18 months but, this time, it was to go into a new business of my own. It was a daunting prospect at 21 years of age to borrow a large amount of money from the bank (after lots of convincing) and to set up a business that hither-to was unheard of: rust-proofing cars. In essence, this entailed spraying and injecting a wax product from

Sweden, called Dinitrol, inside all the boxed-in panels of the car and then under-sealing the full undercarriage. It came with a guarantee, at a time when the only guarantee with a new car was that it was bound to rust – and soon!

I teamed up with my best friend Philip Ferris and, for the next four years, we worked flat out selling this new service, treating cars and doing all these other necessary things you do in a business, like banking, book-keeping, VAT returns, wages, etc. This was what I would call 'jumping in at the deep end' – no experience, no knowledge of whether it would work and a huge learning curve about running a business.

It was hard work but great fun. However, after four years, we both realised we needed more money than we would get from the business to get married, buy houses, support children and so on, so we sold the business as a going concern. Not a huge amount of money made – but no loss either and, to this day, we are both proud of this early achievement and have fond memories of all the things that we did.

My next choice (passion) was to move to a car sales position and I very quickly learned the value of treating employers with respect when I re-applied to PMPA to work as a salesperson. My application was met with an immediate 'Yes' from Joe Moore who was the managing director.

For the next eight years, my life was 'on a roll' – the job was great, I loved selling, I got married, bought a house and had our first three children. In a way, I never wanted this time to end, as it was such fun and so rewarding. I was earning so much from selling that I couldn't leave to take up any of the many management positions in other dealerships that I was offered because I would have had to take a pay cut.

But they say all good things come to an end and, one day, I heard that PMPA Insurance was in financial difficulties and our jobs were in question. Selling is all about confidence and for me to sell a car and tell a customer I would be around to honour a warranty for 12 months was not an option because I didn't know if I would be there next week. It was time to move on.

In 1983, Belgard Motors was then a Renault dealership out in 'the sticks' in Tallaght. I moved there in my first official management role as sales manager. Although my time with Belgard Motors was a brief three years, I have very fond memories and I am still in touch with some of the friends I made there. Little did I realise what was coming down the tracks ... I was offered a position with a large and household name in the industry, Windsor Motors, to become general manager, or in today's language 'dealer principal, of a new branch in South Dublin.

In the mid-1980s, the motor industry was very difficult to make a profit from, as the volume of new car sales was a mere 60,000 cars – less than one-third of the market in 2007 of 186,000 cars. My challenge was to establish this business as a profit centre for an initial period of five years before we relocated and, thankfully, this was achieved. I believe the key to success in those difficult trading times was 'doing the basics brilliantly', which impressed the customers.

This business transferred to Deansgrange in the early 1990s and continued to grow using tried and tested processes, to the point that we could not cater for the volume of business. To deal with the expansion needs, we designed and built a new flagship property in Bray. They say success follows success and I am glad this is true, as Bray became a success from the day it opened. When I consider that this was in a somewhat depressed market and that interest rates exceeded 15% at the time, this was a great tribute to the team who were with me.

Then, out of the blue, the owners of Windsor Motors, Michael and Rita O'Reilly, asked me to take over the management of the entire group which consisted of five dealerships, a car auction business and a car hire company. Now this was the biggest challenge I have ever faced in business and one that was quite daunting for me. To say that I was being challenged 'out of my socks' is an understatement and I was pleased, but petrified, to accept the role of chief executive of the Windsor Motor Group.

I tend not to dwell on mistakes. I don't mind holding my hands up and saying, "I got that one wrong!", and then drawing a line under it and moving on.

My management career had gone from managing a team of 10 staff to 20 to 50 to 150 in a series of reasonably fast moves. It took me a little while to learn that I was no longer the person who did things but was now the person responsible for making sure everything was done by the staff – this was a real change for me. From a nervous start, I set about putting in place the things I knew worked for me elsewhere and, once again, my focus was on 'doing the basics brilliantly' and on establishing a strong customer focus. It has always been my view that it is not the glossy showrooms or the fancy cars that make a business succeed but the staff and all they do for the customer. The staff in Windsor at that time were marvellous and, to this day, I have the highest regard for their abilities and their attitude. I would describe their behaviour as 'professional' and it is these people who get the result that is achieved.

Once again, for me, success followed and, once again, with another new development. Michael and Rita decided to sell the five dealerships to new shareholders. This was not a very visible change to customers and staff; however, for me, it was like starting again, as I had new people to report to.

But the change brought new opportunities and I set a goal to double the business within five years. This was achieved – on time – and I believe we capitalised on a market that was growing and had the capacity for us to grow with it. I have always believed in the power of setting goals and have encouraged so many others within, and outside, Windsor to do the same.

I have also believed in the power of teamwork and the success of everybody pulling together to reach the same goal. The following example of the benefit of teamwork is one I have often used: A Clydesdale horse is a very strong animal and can pull five tons on its own. When two are working together, instead of pulling 10 tons, they can pull 15; when five are working together, instead of pulling 25 tons, they can pull 50! This is a great example of the power of teamwork.

The combined power of setting goals and working together as a team has helped me to continue the growth and development of the company. Today, we have 10 dealerships, a fleet management company, 450 staff and a turnover of €270 million. During my time as chief executive, the staff numbers grew by 90% and profits by 500% - it was a very exciting time in my life and career.

Recently, I took a 'life decision' to retire from this position to create time in my life for other 'passions' outside of business and to hand the reins over to Gabriel Keane who has been working alongside me for the last 10 years. I am pleased to remain with Windsor as a director and continue to have responsibility for certain development projects while I also have time to devote to my other interests.

The best way to 'unwind' is to avoid getting too wound up,
although of course this isn't always easy.

W hat's next? – I'm not sure what will arise just yet but I know it will be good for me and I am looking forward to a continuation of what has been an exciting, challenging and enjoyable career and personal life so far. During my career, I have had many influences and experiences and, for the benefit of any readers who wish to give thought to their career, I will reflect on some of these so that they might give some encouragement or help in forging their own personal goals, passions and visions.

The people you meet along the way are very important to you, as quite often you meet them again and again and it is not unusual that they have also moved on and can help you, so be nice to them!

As an example of this, the person who gave me my first job, nearly 40 years ago, Sean Mooney, became a good friend. However, unfortunately, he had some bad luck in later life and found himself without a job. He walked into the garage that I was running at that time, applied to me for a job and I was privileged to be able to give it to him. So, he gave me my first job and I gave him his last job, as he sadly passed away late last year.

Another example is when I re-applied to PMPA for a job in sales, the answer was positive and immediate. Being good to your employer can pay more than just a salary!

Don't be afraid to make mistakes. Fear holds us back much too often. Now I don't encourage foolishness, or ill-conceived ideas, but I do encourage people to try new ways and new things. Yes, sometimes you will fail but, more often, it is the trier who succeeds. When you do make a mistake, don't be afraid to face it, admit it, even talk about it.

This helps to bring closure and to deal with it and, believe it or not, you are demonstrating courage by doing this.

Set your standards high in everything: your manners, your courtesy, dress standards, work ethic, honesty, etc. This is a 'long-term' decision that will pay dividends and earn you respect from those around you – both above you (boss) and below you (staff) and from your peers.

Give your time to others in a helpful way. Now I don't mean charity, although this is good to do; I mean to help a colleague, a friend, even a competitor sometimes. In my career, I spent time working on a voluntary basis with the motor industry's representative body (the Society of the Irish Motor Industry). Indeed, as a result, I was very honoured in 2003/4 to become president of SIMI and this gave me opportunities to represent the industry, at the highest level in Ireland and other countries. There is as great a pleasure and satisfaction in giving as there is in receiving.

Be true to yourself and follow your passion. This I often refer to as goal-setting. It means you should decide for you what you want to achieve. Believe in yourself. Write down your goal and go for it with 100% commitment. In essence, do the things you want to do and love to do and you will achieve great results and satisfaction.

In this regard, this is my favourite quote from Henry Ford:

> *"Whether you believe you can, or believe you can't, either way you're right."*

Be proud, whether that is of being Irish or doing a good job, proud of your appearance or a sporting achievement. I don't mean to be boastful but, if you take pride in what you do, you will influence those around you in a positive way and this will reflect back to you – positively.

Above all, don't live in the past. Look to the future, plan for the future but live in today. There is a huge power in living in the now! Create as much balance and fun in your life as you can. Meetings don't always have to be serious to be effective – sometimes the jokes turn out to be 'good ideas'. Spend time – as much of it as possible – with your family and friends and have as much fun as possible.

Be a team player!

If you find you are on the wrong track (maybe the wrong job or whatever), don't be afraid to make changes. Some of the world's great people only started working on their passion at a later age, when they were 50 or 60 years old in some cases. So go for what you believe in and don't be afraid – this is what holds you back.

Happiness and contentment are two words that I believe are so important. It's no good being rich and unhappy or discontent, work on what is good for you in the happiness area and life will be good.

Finally, it is one of life's wonderfully fulfilling opportunities to help others. Whether it is your children (and spend lots of time with them), your partner or someone else in the world, I would encourage everybody to do some deed for someone else and to do it without recognition or reward. This will bring its own satisfaction and fulfilment.

*During a recession is probably the best time
to start a business.*

9
PAT MCDONAGH

Pat McDonagh is the founder and managing director of Ireland's most successful indigenous fast-food group, Supermac's, which currently operates 93 restaurants nationwide. It employs over 2,400 people and has established 42 self-employed franchisees in their own successful businesses. In 2006, Pat took on a new venture, Papa John's Pizza.

Pat is married to Una, and they have four children – Marie, Siobhan, John and Conor. He is a very 'hands-on' manager and is highly involved in the day-to-day operation of the company. He is joined on the board of directors by Una, who is also actively involved in all company activities.

Pat is a keen sports fan, in particular the GAA. This love of sport has seen Supermac's sponsor many teams, from the Galway hurling teams to the Irish rowing squads and countless local sports clubs around Ireland. He is also a major supporter of charities and of the arts in Ireland.

The company, which had a turnover of €92 million in 2007, has a policy of actively supporting Irish suppliers where at all possible. This has contributed greatly to the Irish economy in the 30 years since the company was founded. Pat McDonagh has succeeded in an industry where large multinationals are the norm and locally-based chains very much the exception. Where Supermac's has come face-to-face with the multinationals in Ireland, Supermac's invariably has come out on top.

A SCÉIL FHÉIN

I grew up in a little village called Kiltulla, which is near Athenry in Co. Galway. My parents were both civil servants; my father was a Guard in the town, and my mother was a teacher. I attended a local secondary school for a year, but apparently the end-of-year results must have called for drastic action, because then my parents decided to send me to the Carmelite College in Moate, a boarding school, where I stayed for five years. I quite enjoyed my time at the boarding school, although it would not be the sort of education I would choose for my own children. You could call it 'good regimental training'. We were allowed home for the Christmas, Easter and summer holidays, as well as a couple of days at Halloween, but there were certainly no trips home at the weekends. We were expected to work very hard and produce good results and, with the supervised environment that the school offered, that was what we did.

At home, I had done a little bit of hurling but, in the Carmelite College, the emphasis was on Gaelic football, and it was in playing football that I earned my nickname, 'Supermac'. It went like this: one day, our school was playing against St Jarlath's from Tuam. I was having one of my better days, and one of the wags on the sideline came up with the name 'Supermac', and that was how it all started.

During my secondary school years, I did a little part-time and summer work with farmers, and with Bord na Móna. It was then I had my first experience of catering and the food industry when I had a summer job working at Butlin's holiday camp in Mosney. I worked in the bars and in the restaurant, first as a barman, and then as a waiter and a commis chef. Basically, I worked in the kitchens from the ground up, starting out washing dishes, and gradually moving on to more difficult things. After having finished secondary school, however, I decided to follow my mother's advice, which was to get a 'good, government, pensionable job'. I took her example, and qualified as a teacher. I worked in the area for five years, in Limerick, but I always felt that I would do something else. I just couldn't imagine myself spending 40 years teaching.

Sometimes, when your back is to the wall,
it is then that you perform your best,
because you do not have any other option.

O ne of the things I did like about teaching was that the holidays were great, and there was plenty of time off in the evenings, which meant that I could start exploring other options without giving up the safe job, which I was finding increasingly boring. At that time – this was in the early 1970s – a man called Fintan Quinn was setting up pool tables around the country – pool being the fashionable thing at the time. I started using my time off to put pool tables into various pubs and clubs for Fintan and, when he decided to sell out the western part of his business, I bought it and took over from him. I was still teaching when I found and acquired premises on Main Street in Ballinasloe. I felt that the premises would lend itself perfectly to becoming an amusement centre and pool hall, and I applied for planning permission for the same. Unfortunately – or fortunately, as things turned out – the planning authorities did not agree with me. Now I was left with a venue, and no clue as to what I was going to do with it. I sat down and thought about what Ballinasloe needed, about what was missing from the town. Two things came to mind: a fast-food restaurant and a furniture shop.

At that time, McDonald's and Burger King had just arrived in Dublin, and it seemed as though fast-food was going to be the next big thing, so I decided that I would open my own fast-food restaurant, now that the pool hall was out of the question. I divided the shop space in half, letting one-half out to a fashion shop called Michael Ward Fashions, which still trades successfully to this day across the road from the original Supermac's. I fixed the other half up to function as a fast-food restaurant, to which I gave my own nickname. That was the start of Supermac's.

Although I had gained some experience in catering when I was a young lad working in Butlin's, I didn't know very much about it, and certainly not enough to run my own fast-food restaurant. So I hired a chef called Michael Carroll to teach us what we would need to know to get started. Michael was a chef in Hayden's Hotel, a very fine establishment in the town at the time. Our first restaurant opened in 1978 to serve the people of Ballinasloe, who didn't realise that they were being used as guinea pigs to find out what would sell and what wouldn't! Having had no real experience in business at all, for me the early years were a case of trial and error and I had to learn quickly and on my feet to keep everything up and running.

After about six months of running Supermac's, I decided that it was time to commit to one thing or the other, so I went to Fr. Kirby (now Bishop) to give my notice and inform him that I would not be teaching any more. When he asked me why, I told him that it seemed to me that there was more money in chips than in algebra. He accepted my resignation.

What I found is that you learn as much from the street and from dealing with people as you do from books or whatever. You have to learn as you go along because, if you do not, you won't survive.

I still remember the famous Ballinasloe fair, our first year in business. The fair, a huge horse fair that attracts tens of thousands of participants, is the largest in Europe; it is the biggest social event every year in the town. Everyone in Ballinasloe told me that it would be the biggest commercial event of the year as well, so we got in extra supplies and staff and were ready to go … or so we thought. Everything was in full swing, when, at about half past midnight, we lost all our power. The main fuse was gone, presumably because our electrician hadn't thought about or catered for times of heavy usage. So, there we were in the dark, with 100 hungry customers waiting to be fed. They all had had a lot to drink and weren't particularly patient, so it was now a situation of some urgency. I got a pair of pliers, plucked out the fuse, taped a piece of cigarette paper around the two ends and stuck it back in again. A few sparks flew, but it held together for an hour or so and we continued to feed the hungry. When it went again, I fished it out, and repaired it with tin-foil. We managed to keep feeding customers until about half past three in the morning, when the whole street went dark. I never told the ESB what had happened but, as we have paid them very well ever since, I think that I will probably be forgiven!

The year after we opened, 1979, Pope John Paul came on an official visit to Ireland. From a business point of view, this was a unique event. Just at Ballybrit alone, there were 250,000 people to hear the Pope say Mass. Mass was supposed to end at about 2.00pm, so I expected a hungry crowd to arrive back at Ballinasloe at about 3pm. We prepared our staff to be ready for the onslaught at 3.30 or 4.00pm, but I came in on my own to open up and get things ready. As it turned out, the Pope finished up rather earlier than expected and, long before my staff arrived for work, I found myself facing a large, if orderly, queue that stretched down the street. The joys of business! I did the best I could, having reduced the menu to just sausages and chips, and two curious Gardaí, popping in to see what was happening, declined my suggestion that they get behind the counter to help.

Another mistake that I made in the early years was to buy what appeared to be wonderful potatoes from a new supplier, when our regular supplier ran out at Christmas time, and we had to arrange an alternative in a hurry. The new ones were called 'Aran Banners', and their moisture content was so high that they made dreadful chips; so bad, I was embarrassed handing them out that weekend.

Later, I found out that Aran Banner potatoes are really only suitable for use as cattle feed. On the spot, we had to decide that it was time to switch to frozen chips, and that's the way we've gone since. In any business, one soon learns the importance of thinking on one's feet!

The culture is different, it is changing constantly and there are always new things that we have to stay on top of, to be aware of.

Although I had had various summer jobs in my youth, I had no real business experience at all before setting up on my own, and no formal business training at university. Looking back, I'm not sure whether this was a good or a bad thing. I was ignorant of the problems that lay ahead, yet I didn't get put off starting anything.

So I suppose it definitely had its advantages. In other ways, I suppose it held me back, because I wasn't able to make educated decisions of the sort that business training might have assisted with. Over the years, however, I found out that one learns at least as much from just dealing with people and being 'on the street'. To survive, it is absolutely essential to keep learning all the time, and to become able to transform difficulties along the way into positives.

The culture of business has changed a lot in Ireland since I set up in the 1970s, and in various different ways. For one thing, we have an inordinate number of rules and regulations now, to do with planning, employment law, health and safety, and so forth. Many of these rules are good and worthwhile, but has it all gone a bit overboard by this stage? Nowadays, managers spend 20% of their time filling out forms and checklists to comply with the law, although most of this paperwork will be left in filing cabinets and computers, and never seen again. I think that Ireland is probably even more heavily regulated than the United States, and it is over-regulated.

A successful business is also built on customer service,
as I expect you'll have heard from other business people.
Good customer service is key to doing well.

S upermac's has grown a lot since I set it up; we now have over 90 branches all over the country, including several in the North. For me, keeping motivated and excited about doing business means constantly looking out for something new, whether in different aspects of the food or leisure business or something else. It's crucial to keep one's eye on what is happening down the line. For this reason, the organisation has grown to include more than just Supermac's. A few years ago, we got involved in a pub and restaurant business in the United States, the Claddagh Irish Pubs. The first pubs opened in 2000. Although they are designed as pubs, most of the revenue is generated from the provision of food. Essentially, these are Irish restaurants serving the United States. I still see the United States in general very much as a land of opportunity for Irish business people, considering just how many Americans claim Irish ancestry, and how deep their affinity with Ireland is. There are almost 400 million Americans, which makes the potential market truly enormous. In our case, we really wanted to see how our idea of setting up Irish restaurants would work out, and initially they did very well indeed. For a while, we took our eye off the ball and made a few mistakes, such as expanding too quickly, and things started to slow down, but we are focussing on them again now and, if I had to describe my proudest achievement, it would be turning them around, which I expect to achieve in the course of the next 18 months. Perhaps if anything marks me out as an entrepreneur, it's feeling proudest of what I've yet to achieve!

The things that you have to have to be successful are
attitude and teamwork. It sounds like a cliché but it is true.

H ere in Ireland, we also have gone beyond just Supermac's. For example, we recently took out a franchise for Papa John's Pizza Delivery. Papa John's is an American pizza delivery business, with franchises around the world. At present, we have nine outlets in operation, since its start-up only two years ago, so the business is still in its infancy. Starting any new business is a steep learning curve. One might think that the food business is all more or less the same but, with pizza delivery, it's less about the food and more about the logistics of making sure that deliveries get out on time, and arrive in good condition. While Papa John's is still very much at a preliminary stage in Ireland, it is growing well, and we expect it to grow a lot quickly, so there's plenty of work to do there!

The Irish are naturally good communicators,
whether it is because of our culture or …
a question of natural ability, or for whatever reason.

I have already mentioned some of the mistakes I've made over the years, and making mistakes is inevitable. However, one of the most important ways a business can cope with problems and keep moving forward successfully is by building good teams. With a good team, a business can always be carried forward. Selecting the right people is the key to team-building. Finding exactly the right people to work with is difficult, but it is absolutely essential in an expanding business. I can speak from experience: in the past, for example, there have been times when I may have allowed things to become somewhat overextended, without making sure that we had the people back-up that we needed. Another thing that is crucial at all times is to have a very good relationship with one's bank, so that it can be counted on for support when the business needs it. For instance, at one time I thought that I had a very good relationship with the bank that I was dealing with and, for that reason, bought a very high-profile premises, assuming my bank would back me up and that the financial support would be all in place. At the last moment, I was informed that my bank was not going to stand behind me on this particular project at all. I had my back to the wall. Fortunately, these are the circumstances when one often performs best, in the absence of any other option. Anyone who wants to stay in business just has to get the wherewithal together to make things happen, even when circumstances conspire against them. In this case, I had to gather my thoughts quickly, and find another bank that was anxious to do business with us. In fact, we had done some business on a small scale with the second bank before, so I went to them with a small white lie, and told them that this was their chance to get on board, because there were other offers on the table. Fortunately for all concerned, they did get on board, and I have been doing business with them ever since; I hope they don't regret their decision! Having a good relationship with one's bank pays off in difficult times. In 1988, for example, a lot of businesses had a very stressful period, because there was an enormous hike in interest rates, and many were paying more than 20%, which proved to be quite unsustainable in some cases.

In difficult times, successful business people do what they must to enable themselves to make a plan, present it to whomever they are dealing with, and come out with a deal. I have already mentioned the huge importance of teamwork. However, personal attitude is also enormously important. While it can be acquired, to some extent, by people who are working in an organisation with a good culture, and a good atmosphere of teamwork, I am not sure that it can be learned. You either have it or you don't.

Another very difficult time for our business was in the early 2000s, when it became fashionable to present Supermac's and other businesses with fraudulent insurance claims. We suffered a lot from this for a number of years. Basically, a small number of members of the public decided that it would be clever to fake 'incidents' resulting in injury on our premises, and to sue Supermac's. The legal profession also did quite nicely from the whole proceedings, and my feeling is that lawyers and solicitors promoted this to some extent as well, at the expense of Supermac's and other businesses. For a while, the whole thing was getting quite out of control, with a claim once a month against our branch on O'Connell Street in Dublin alone. Of course, this became quite a serious financial drain on our organisation, although the cases were clearly fraudulent.

Any successful business has to be able to adapt to the changing times and, to do that, it needs to be aware of shifts in the culture and expectations of its customer base. In our case, many of our customers are children and families, and we need to be aware of the constant changes in popular culture, as these are very relevant to the way we present our business and to the provisions we provide them with. For example, children today have very different expectations and lifestyles than a number of years ago. They have X-boxes, and they play video games, and so forth, and these things influence all their tastes and responses to their environment, including the fast-food restaurants they visit. Consequently, we need to work hard to keep our restaurants up-to-date, so that they always look fresh, contemporary, and appealing to these key customers so that they will want their parents to take them there, and that they will want to return. Also, with respect to menus, we need to be sensitive to changes in our customers' tastes and preferences, and keep menus new so that our customers do not get bored of what we have to offer. People today are much more health-conscious than they would have been in the past, and we have had to respond to this by including different items on our Supermac's menus. In the case of Papa John's, our pizza delivery service, we are also rising to meet changes in Irish culture that have emerged in recent years. What's relevant to how we present Papa John's to the Irish public is the growing tendency of customers to stay in and order food to be delivered to their homes, rather than going out. Home delivery services is now the new trend.

The key to running a successful business in any industry is customer service. Good customer service is indispensable, because when one's customers are happy, they will return and buy again, and the business will grow.

It is probably one of the most difficult parts of expanding any business, to build a team around you that is going to move forward with you.

Rather than admiring one specific Irish businessperson, I find inspiration in many, and I am also inspired by business people outside the Irish milieu.

Consider the case of Ingvar Kamprad from Sweden, for example. Although he is dyslexic, and has serious problems with reading and writing, Ingvar Kamprad founded IKEA, the furniture retailer, which has become one of the most successful organisations in the world.

Within Ireland, I have a lot of respect for Louis Fitzgerald, the publican and hotelier. I also have a lot of admiration for Feargal Quinn of Superquinn and Padraig Ó Céidigh of Aer Arann, among others.

With regard to the future, the future of business in Ireland … the future of entrepreneurship … I would say that the future of entrepreneurship in Ireland is in all probability foreign-born, especially in the catering business.

Personally, I feel that one of the great strengths of the Irish, when it comes to business, is the whole area of sales and marketing. The Irish are very strong in these fields. We are naturally good communicators, whether it's because of our culture or for another reason, Irish people are good at getting their point across.

Another factor in our favour is an historical one; nobody hates the Irish, because we never colonised or waged war on anybody! Moreover, in just about every war there has been, there have been Irish people fighting on every side. Around the world, people have a generally favourable view of the Irish, which is very helpful in terms of doing business internationally.

However, if I am to guess where the future of entrepreneurship in Ireland lies, I would say that it is foreign-born rather than Irish-born. Particularly in the catering and hospitality industries today, immigrants who have come to Ireland from overseas to work in recent years are carrying out most of the work in the service industry. The vast majority of these people are very industrious and very ambitious, and they are prepared to start at the bottom and work their way up, whereas their Irish counterparts have become accustomed to receiving large salaries, and are less inclined to assume risk, which makes them less entrepreneurial in spirit. Many young Irish people starting in business today do not remember times when making money was infinitely more difficult. With the challenge of setting up their own business, with all the associated risks, it may look overwhelming to them. It is likely, however, that gradually we will see more and more of our foreign-born counterparts doing extremely well, and becoming the entrepreneurs of tomorrow—particularly, as I said, in the fields of catering, food and hospitality.

You have to come up with a plan yourself, and then find the wherewithal to go and present it to whoever you are dealing with and come out with a deal at the end of it.

I do enjoy things outside work, such as the GAA, rugby and sport in general, but I am not sure how good I really am at achieving a balance between life and work. I enjoy what I do.

To speak for myself, one of the things that motivates me most is getting up in the morning, and always having something new and exciting to do. This was why I originally decided to give up teaching and go into business on my own. It's why we embrace new experiences, such as the Papa John's franchise, and the Claddagh pubs and restaurants in the United States. There is always a new challenge to face, and this is why my business keeps expanding.

Certainly, I always enjoy the challenge of doing something new, of getting up in the morning and having something new, something exciting, to attend to.

10
PADRAIG Ó CÉIDIGH

Padraig Ó Céidigh is the quintessential entrepreneur. At 10, the Connemara-born Ó Céidigh was picking periwinkles from a beach in Spiddal and travelling to Galway to sell them to fish exporters.

He originally trained as a teacher, then started to work as an accountant with KMPG and studied law at night. In 1993, he set up his own legal practice in Galway. A year later, he became part owner of the then loss-making Aer Arann, an airline that served the three Aran Islands. By the time he had taken full control of the airline, he had driven it back into profitability. Aer Arann has grown its passenger numbers from 8,000 in 1999 to over 600,000 in 2007 and is now the third busiest carrier out of Dublin airport.

One of the fastest-growing regional airlines in Europe, Aer Arann is the current sponsor of the Galway Senior Football team and the Connacht Senior Rugby team. Aer Arann was awarded the *European Bronze Airline of the Year Award* for 2004 by the European Regions Airline Association.

Ó Céidigh has also established *Foinse*, one of the country's best-selling Irish language newspapers. He is the owner of a printing company, Clódóirí Lurgan Teo, based in Connemara, as well as a local summer language school. In 2003, Padraig was appointed to the board of Fáilte Ireland.

Padraig and Aer Arann also actively support local and national charities, having raised over €400,000 in the past five years by organising and sponsoring an annual half marathon on the island of Inis Mór.

A former winner of the Ernst & Young *Entrepreneur of the Year* competition, Padraig is currently a member of the *Irish Entrepreneur of the Year* judging panel, and was a member of the 2004 *World Entrepreneur of the Year* judging panel. In spite of all this, he still remembers how to pick periwinkles!

A SCÉIL FHÉIN

I grew up in Spiddal, Connemara in an Irish-speaking, working class family. I remember spending a lot of time picking periwinkles at the sea as a child, and working on the bog. Irish was my first language, and I started learning English only when I began attending my local primary school. I went to the 'Jes' secondary school, *Coláiste Iognáid*, in Galway City, purely because that was where my best friend was going. At the time, I was hoping to become a plumber, but the headmaster spoke to my father and mother and said, "Jaysus, don't let that fellow become a plumber. He should go to college and get a degree".

Following the headmaster's advice, I did a degree in Commerce at University College Galway, and went on to work in accountancy with KPMG. After a few years, I needed a change. First, I returned to teach in my old secondary school, where I stayed for several years. Later, I set up a law practice. That went well, and I sold the practice in the early 1990s, when I bought Aer Arann in partnership with a friend and started building up the airline.

The crucial thing is to enjoy where you are going.
If you enjoy the journey, it is irrelevant whether you
actually reach your original destination.

L ooking back, I can see very clearly that the university training I received was completely irrelevant to any success I have enjoyed in business later on. Fortunately, the quality of business education has improved and I think that young people in university today are receiving a better grounding in business than was the case in my day, although universities still have a long way to go. I created some controversy a few years ago when I was speaking at a university forum in Dublin and said to the assembled university professors: "Look at it in business terms. You provide a product for a society that no longer exists." The simple fact is that too many colleges are still teaching things that are no longer relevant, and endlessly writing clever articles based on other people's clever articles, which will only be read by academics, but have no usefulness or application in the real world.

Still, universities are getting better at interacting with business. I'm executive chair of the MBA programme at the University in Galway. In America, places like Stanford and Kellogg are very connected with business, and in the United States successful business people, some of whom might not have had any university education at all, but have the gumption, know-how and 'street-wise-ness' to go out and actually do it, are brought in to teach in conjunction with the academics. The best learning environments are created when business people from around the world can get together.

In any company, it's better to have just one person calling the shots, whether they are calling them right or calling them wrong.

I have no particular interest in airlines or aeroplanes. To me, planes are just buses with wings and serve merely to take passengers from one place to another. My involvement in the industry started when I was in my wife's family's place one Christmas day, in Currenroan, beside *An Poitín Stil* bar in Connemara. On a long walk that afternoon, I came across a half-finished runway in the middle of nowhere. It was around four o'clock in the evening, getting dark, and it all seemed magical and amazing. Who could be building an airstrip in the middle of a bog in Connemara?

I found out that it was a man called Tom Kilroe, from Roscommon. Tom had gone over to Manchester when he was 16 years old without a penny in his pocket and had become one of the richest Irishmen in the UK. Now, he was thinking of selling Aer Arann but, when I told him a bit about myself, he told me not to waste his time, because there was no way I could afford to buy an airline. He was right, but that didn't stop me! Somehow, I managed to put the money together, going into partnership and re-mortgaging my house.

At that time, Aer Arann had an annual turnover of about €250,000; now it's at about €110 million a year. Then, we had about eight staff, and now we have between 500 and 550, mostly in our offices in Dublin. Our passenger numbers have grown from the relatively small number of people travelling to the Aran Islands to about 1.2 million travelling within Ireland and to other destinations, so it's grown quite a lot in the last few years. Between 1994/5 and 2001, the turnover grew steadily to about €3 million, which was good but not sensational. Then 9/11 happened. That was a difficult time for airlines in general and, at Aer Arann, our back was to the wall. In fact, the company was on the verge of going under. My partner wanted out, so I bought his share. Over the years that followed, turnover went from €3 million to a €110 million. It was easier having just one person in charge; in any company, it's better to have just one person calling the shots, whether they are calling them right or calling them wrong.

Aer Arann's customers vary from route to route, but I can generalise by saying that we serve both business people and tourists, with some statistical variation from one season to another. I would describe Aer Arann as being 'relatively successful' and no more than that. In fact, I see Aer Arann as fundamentally unsuccessful in certain respects for a number of reasons. For one, air travel is a very high-risk industry. In 2007, the air industry in general made a profit of 0.5%. Then again, the sector that we are in, the regional market, is an even higher risk industry to be in. Airlines are very vulnerable to changes in the global economy. At the moment, in early 2008, fuel is terribly expensive at $125 a barrel, up from $22 in 2001. There's constant downward pressure on fares, while wages and salaries and airport charges don't go down. At Aer Arann, we are constantly manoeuvring and changing just to survive and keep going, making success a relative quantity.

I have never had a mentor in business, unfortunately, although there have often been times when that would have been useful! At Aer Arann, my partner and I did have a Board of Directors, which offered advice at various times. In 2001, the chairman of Aer Arann advised that we were lacking a chief executive, and proposed that I fill the role. The company was not doing well, and it needed someone at the helm. Initially, I was very reluctant, but I agreed that I would be CEO for 12 months. In the event, I stayed until 2006.

Honestly, leading and trying to develop a company often was desperately lonely. There I was, with two planes flying to the Aran Islands, saying, "I'm going to be Ireland's internal airline!". I didn't know anything about airlines, I didn't have any money, I didn't have the staff for it and the banks wouldn't support me. I looked like a dreamer and a fool, and I was on my own. The only person I had to talk to in difficult times was my wife but, after a while, I realised it wasn't fair to burden her with the problems at work. Fortunately, I had some really good staff, and we became extremely close.

> *I never had a mentor and, to tell the truth, I found it very
> lonely, trying to lead and develop a company.*

From my own experience, and from what I have seen, I think that we in Ireland need to work much harder at ensuring proper mentoring for business people in the early stages of their career. By 'mentors', I refer to women and men who have proper, proven track records of achievement, because they have started their own businesses and grown them. As a rule of thumb, I would suggest than any enterprise with a turnover of €1 million or so should have a Board of Directors of about three people who are qualified to advise and who would meet regularly to give direction to the entrepreneur. I would also propose that, when grants are given, they are spent on covering the costs of these directors and on mentoring in general.

Giving money to 'create employment' is of very limited benefit, and giving money to buy equipment is similarly limited, as we have seen in Ireland over and over again. Instead, investing in those individual business people who have the gumption and talent to develop new enterprises will pay dividends. The best way to invest in them is to make the advice they need accessible to them. Furthermore, I propose that the top performers—the business people with most potential—in each region should be supported financially and otherwise in their training as individuals and as business people, because these are the people who will create opportunities in Ireland.

In his book *The Tipping Point*, Malcolm Gladwell maintains that a very small number of people have enormous potential and influence in their communities, and have the ability to create differences. These are the people who are leaders, and who are looked up to. We in Ireland need to identify these people and ask ourselves how we can help them grow, because they are the ones who will create new opportunities and will give jobs to everyone else. Currently, most support for training is given to employees on lower pay and, while this is useful, we need much, much more support for the individuals who employ them.

When I won the *Ernst & Young Entrepreneur of the Year* in 2002, I was asked whether I could be interviewed in my office. At the time, the office was just a scruffy prefab, and initially I was horrified at the thought of having to show it to the journalists. In the event, representing Ireland in the *World Entrepreneur of the Year* event in Monte Carlo in 2003 was a very humbling experience, and I felt proud and privileged to be there. To represent your country in any discipline is an honour and I feel very privileged to have been chosen to have done so.

As Aer Arann continued to grow, we needed to change the skill-sets available to the company, which resulted in many new staff being hired at the head office in Dublin. A company is like a football team. A team that's great in the second division isn't necessarily going to be able to play in the first division. In about 2004, I looked at where the company was, where I wanted to bring it to and how I was going to bring it there. I looked at the skills available in the company and started by looking at myself and asking whether I had the qualities necessary in a CEO who would bring Aer Arann from where it was to where I wanted it to go. I realised that I didn't tick a lot of the boxes for the CEO if the company was to achieve what I wanted it to.

"Alright, Padraig", I said to myself, "Call yourself ashore first. If you're not the right person you need to find the man or woman who is". That's how I found Gary Cullen, who is now the CEO, and who has skills that I don't have. Any company leader needs to be prepared to do to themselves what they ask of their employees. I knew that Gary would do a better job than me, and I feel that my stepping down sent a strong message to the staff, that maybe they should start looking at their own skills and ask, "Where am I at? What could I do?". People who are not prepared to leave situations that they are not completely qualified for do so because of ego, and because they do not want to relinquish power and control. Those who are driven by these things rather than the best interests of the company are on the wrong horse, in my view.

Now, in 2008, I remain the chairman of the Board of Aer Arann, which is not a full-time executive position. However, I remain very active in working on the strategy and vision of the company. The role of the management team is to develop and execute the strategy, and they are in a much better position than me to do so.

> *I constantly work on changing my own skills.*
> *I am always learning and seeking learning situations.*
> *I love learning and seeing how one could do things*
> *differently and better.*

I am very aware that what I don't know about business is infinite, while what I do know is minimal. Every year, I take three or four weeks out and I do a business retreat, because I have so much to learn and I like to upgrade my knowledge continuously. I constantly try to develop my skills and discover different, more effective ways of doing things. It is also essential to know how to learn from mistakes. Over the years, I have often made the mistake of taking people at their word, when some people will always try to mislead or will be less than straightforward. Now, we have systems and processes within the company to prevent these issues, and we're a very strong company as a result.

Goals change, and one needs to adapt to those changes. When I took over Aer Arann, my goal was simply to provide a safe, reliable and profitable service to the Aran Islands. We achieved that very quickly, and I could see that there was still a very big gap in the market for flying around Ireland. Then we decided that, even if we weren't going to be the biggest regional airline in Europe, we'd be the best, and we started working towards that goal. We achieved that, too. We received the *Palme d'Or* award; only the second time in six years of the competition that this has been given to an airline. In Dublin, we won the *Sean F. Lemass* award from the Marketing Institute of Ireland. So I suppose we were doing something right.

One of Aer Arann's main strengths is customer service. We know from customer feedback that 92% would fly again with us, and would recommend us to a friend. Customer service is the factor that differentiates us from our main competitor, which at the moment is Ryanair. We maintain high standards in this area, both by providing training within the company and, more importantly, by establishing a general culture of customer service within the organisation. Part of that involves taking care of staff, so that they in turn will look after the customers. I believe in giving people responsibility and considerable autonomy within their position. In return, they become part of the culture. For example, a gentleman called Tom Colgan started working with us when he was 60 or so. Previously, he had been employed as an engineer by Aer Lingus. When he reached retirement age, Tom came to me and said, "The last three and a half years in Aer Arann were more enjoyable than the 30-odd years I spent with Aer Lingus. There, I was fixing planes; in Aer Arann, I was building an airline".

In any company, the person who has the greatest influence on defining culture is the leader, so their personality, and what they live and breathe, what they believe, and what their core values are, all are central. If the well-being of people is a core aspect of the leader of the company, there's a much stronger chance that this will become a core value of the organisation in general. Also, leaders will tend to employ people with similar core values, and those people will do likewise, until a certain set of values pervades the organisation.

At the same time, training is hugely important. We have what we call the 'Aer Arann University', which is a system within the company whereby each member goes through a structured training programme.

At the core of our approach is that people matter,
and that our customers are number one.
Also, you're not going to provide a world class service to
customers unless you have a world class team.

A bout five years ago, someone told me that I was a 'serial entrepreneur'. At the time, I thought it sounded like a disease, and actually I think it *is* a kind of disease. A serial entrepreneur is someone who enjoys a challenge, but gets bored when a goal has been achieved, and needs to do something else. Achievement is not what drives them; when they've achieved a goal they get bored and want to go and try something else. What they really enjoy is the process of pushing and getting there and I think that's also true of activities not directly related to work.

Speaking for myself, I have been involved over the years in various marathons and mini-marathons to raise funds for charity. For me, the satisfaction in running a marathon lies in actually in going and running it, although there's often pain and you're going uphill and it's raining and so forth, rather than necessarily finishing it at the end. You reach a point when you're feeling sorry for yourself and you decide to give yourself a kick in the ass and you just keep going through it. When it's over, you think, "Now I want to go and do it again!".

I focus on the journey; I've never looked long term. In fact, in business and in life, I think it can be dangerous to look too much at the long term.

I believe that, in business and in life, it can be dangerous to look too much at the long term. Planning is hugely important, but so is flexibility. I try to focus from month to month and year to year. Of course, five- and 10-year plans can be enormously helpful, but one can be sure that, whatever happens, things won't work out as they were written up in the original plan! Most often, people who write down their plans and goals and work towards achieving them achieve far more than they originally set out to do. I keep structure in my life and work by having a weekly diary, a monthly diary and a three-monthly diary. I look at them often and stay on top of what I need to do, but I remain flexible. We all need to look at how we are distributing our energy, and to know whether or not we are putting it in the right places.

So, have a plan. But look at it constantly, and constantly
change it.

There are obstacles to business and entrepreneurship in Ireland today, and I feel that one is the loss of our spiritual side. In all areas of endeavour, people need to be strong mentally, emotionally and spiritually. If any one of these issues is off-balance, it pulls the rest out of sync and the resulting problems impact on both personal and professional life. Similarly, physical well-being is essential. A deficit in any of these areas will impact negatively on anyone and on their business and everyone they work with.

For company leaders, it is essential that they work hard at establishing personal equilibrium before demanding the same of others. With respect to what I see as a spiritual deficit in Irish culture, I've become involved in the early stages of developing a dedicated centre of spiritual excellence in Ireland, where people will be able to spend time in a completely different environment now and again.

I'm also involved professionally in a number of areas, including alternative energy, an Irish language newspaper, *Foinse*, and various others. Also, cognisant of the fact that I would have found a mentor personally very helpful, I have become involved in a mentoring relationship with a number of young people who are starting out in business. It's nothing formal; they phone up every now again and we have a chat, or we meet three or four times a year. A lot of people ask me for business advice and I don't try to help everyone, but I do stay in contact with a few people. Mostly, young entrepreneurs already know the answers to their own questions, but having someone help them voice those answers is very helpful.

I always look outside my industry for ideas.
I'm not going to learn inside it.

H aving the right attitude is fundamental to having a successful business. One of the things I've learned is that attitude is hard to change. Skills can always be acquired, but turning attitudes around is a real challenge. While, in general, Irish culture is more positive than ever before towards entrepreneurship, when an individual, a business or a company doesn't achieve success, too many hurlers on the ditch are still prepared to say, "Arra, I knew it wouldn't work!".

Unfortunately, this is all too common in the media, and it is not good for our culture or business environment in general. Some sections of the Irish media are not always very professional or objective, and they do love to focus almost exclusively on the negative.

Attitude, skill and talent are all important ...
attitude is an internal thing in terms of how staff see
things, get things done and behave as part of a team.
But they have to have the talent as well.

W hile I cannot identify one single person as a particular source of inspiration, I am full of admiration for anyone, in whatever area, who feels able to battle their way upstream, whether their business is a grocery shop or a pub or whatever. These are the people who make a difference in their own and others' lives, and the state of their bank balance is irrelevant. These are the people who make Ireland a better place for themselves, their families and others. One of the most important contributions they make is the creation of jobs. With a job, a source of income, people have integrity, independence and the ability to create their own destiny.

For me, marketing is quite simple. It means, first of all,
knowing about your product, and knowing where that
product and service creates value added, and what value
added to which segments of the population.

I reland has changed hugely in recent years with respect to entrepreneurship. As recently as the 1990s, entrepreneurs were frowned upon and seen as 'chancers'. However, from the early years of the new millennium, entrepreneurship became very popular. Now it's seen as a vital ingredient of any economy, especially a small, open economy like Ireland's. We have to acknowledge that various governments helped, in creating the lower corporation tax climate, in creating stability in the various agreements with trade unions and in stabilising employment situations. Nor should we underestimate the role of the peace process in Northern Ireland, which has yet to continue translating into economic and financial gain. Also, for various reasons, the Irish people in general are much more confident than we were. Now, thanks largely to the huge growth in our economy in a short period, we believe in our own talents and abilities and we believe that we're as good as any other nation in the world. Of course, Ireland is part of a world economy, and will be affected by economic ebbs and flows, but I am very confident that there are many more opportunities for success in entrepreneurship than obstacles to it. In any case, true entrepreneurs are happy working in recession as well as in boom economic environments, because they understand risk, and they know that recessions create better opportunities.

Ireland does not have a long history in terms of driving new businesses, although it is well-placed with respect to opportunities for all its citizens when compared to many emerging economies. We remain much too dependent on American and other foreign multinationals coming in and telling us what to do and how to do it. Although our confidence is greater than ever before, we spent generations thinking, "We can't do that". Although entrepreneurship does now have a foothold here, it is not yet as deeply entrenched as it needs to be. I have no doubt that we will get there, however, because Ireland has created the fundamental qualities for future development.

Nonetheless, we need to work on bringing our transport systems up to acceptable standards and on improving our health system. We also need to help our banks to provide better support, because currently many banks do not understand businesses and businesspeople well enough, particularly in the early days of an enterprise. Banks are not good at deciding who should be supported and who should not, and this is a significant disadvantage to Irish businesses starting up. Despite these setbacks, all the basics are solid. What is crucial at the current moment is that we need to work on our collective weaknesses effectively and very quickly, because they are impeding our economic growth and success from an economic perspective.

We need to be in a position to replace the big American companies, which will continue to drift overseas. We will have to create our own innovation, and conduct our own customer and product research. We will have to be creative!

Key to success is constantly striving to do things differently and better, and one can learn a lot outside one's specific industry. Just looking inside the same industry can result in similar products or services being created over and over again by different people. It's like photocopying; the result is the same, but weaker, than the original. I always look outside my industry for ideas. I'm not going to learn inside it.

Entrepreneurs prefer to work when the economy is in recession, because the recession creates better opportunities.

I rish people are blessed with good social and communication skills, but we do not generally excel at marketing. I would say that our marketing skills are average, at best, because we frequently confuse 'marketing' and 'selling', and tend to imitate what is done in other parts of Ireland and in other countries, rather than innovating. We often abdicate responsibility for marketing, because we don't really understand it or what's involved.

For me, marketing is quite simple. It means, first of all, knowing about your product, and knowing where that product and service creates value added, and what value added means for which segments of the population. It is a question of establishing your market, and connecting your product to your marketing in such a way that value is added to the product or service. Of course, pricing, advertising and promotion all come into that, but Irish business people often fail to understand the value, if any, that they give to any section of the market, and this questions the sustainability of the product or service.

I don't think that Irish people are naturally good marketers, although they have good social and good communication skills.

O f course, it is important to find a balance between 'work' and 'life'. I genuinely relax doing business, a lot of the time, and I am a lot more relaxed than I was, now that I have a good management team in Dublin. Apart from business, I relax by running marathons and half-marathons. I've run the New York marathon three times and I've done about 15 half-marathons. Generally, I run two or three times a week, and go to the gym two or three times a week, to balance out the 70 or so hours I spend doing business in an average week. I manage to spend much more time with my family than I did before, and I have plans to do other things that are not related to work, such as upgrading my accordion-playing skills.

I think that a balance between life and work is very important ... People need to be strong mentally, emotionally and spiritually and, if any of those qualities is off-balance, it pulls the rest out of sync.

I 'm always aware that Aer Arann faces serious challenges, and that nothing is certain but, as I said, being an entrepreneur is about the journey, not the destination. The crucial thing is to enjoy where you are going. If you enjoy the journey, it is irrelevant whether you actually reach your original destination.

*While I don't have any one person in particular to look up
to, I really admire anybody and everybody who's able to
jump out of their comfort zone and
not feel afraid to swim and battle their way upstream.*

11
FEARGAL QUINN

Senator Feargal Quinn is President of EuroCommerce, the Brussels-based retail, wholesale and international trade representation to the EU.

He is also President of Superquinn, an independent Irish supermarket company that he founded in 1960. Superquinn, a private company, operates 22 supermarkets and nine shopping centres.

Apart from his involvement with Superquinn, Feargal Quinn has made many other contributions to Irish life. Most prominently, he was chairman of Ireland's national postal service for 10 years. He chaired a steering committee on the reform of a key element in Ireland's education system and was chairman of the St. Patrick's Day Festival. Since 1993, he has been an independent member of Seanad Éireann. He has received three honorary doctorates from Irish educational institutions and a Papal Knighthood.

Senator Quinn serves on the board of directors of CIES – the Food Business Forum, based in Paris, and the American-based Food Marketing Institute.

A SCÉIL FHÉIN

My mother came from County Armagh, and my father from County Down. They met through the Post Office. Dad was from Newry, and he would phone home *via* the exchange in Dun Laoghaire. This was in about 1930, when you gave the number to an operator. My father noticed that his operator had a Northern accent and, on the third phone call or so, they started to chat, and he actually made a blind date with her. Then he got worried! He went down to the post office, and found that there were three women behind the counter; an "auld one, an ugly one and a smasher". He went in and bought a two-penny stamp from the old one, and she had a Cork accent. Then he went and bought one from the plain one, and she had a Dublin accent. Well, then he knew that the smasher was the Northern girl, and that was how it all started. My sister and I grew up not far from Dun Laoghaire, in Blackrock.

My father had gone to America during the Irish War of Independence, at 17 years of age. He had returned at 22, but despite deciding to settle in Ireland, he was very pro-American all his life, and my sister and I grew up very aware of the American way of living and doing business. Dad's family had been in the grocery business, and Dad worked in the same area until I was about nine, when he left the field and opened the Red Island Holiday Camp in Skerries, County Dublin. Almost all the guests, about 500 at a time, came from 'across the water': England, Scotland and Wales. That was where I got my earliest business experience, as a 10-year-old shoeshine boy, and my earliest exposure to the concept of making your customer happy, even if that means not extracting as much money from them as you possibly can at first contact. Later, I was given a microphone to call out the bingo numbers, and I learned about the importance of humour. The idea at Red Island was not to sell your customer something, but to get customers to return next year by making sure that they were happy. Often, when they left, customers would shake my father's hand and say, "I've had a great time, and I'll be back again next year!". My father was my first mentor in business, and probably the most influential.

Certainly, I always tried to instil in the people who worked with me at Superquinn the approach to customers that I learned from him.

Trying out something new that doesn't work out is fine;
the real failure is not even trying.

D uring term times, I attended the Dominican College in Newbridge. There were about 50 students in my year at school, and I was the only one who was then planning to go into business. The idea in the 1950s was that the important thing was to get a good, safe, pensionable job. Ireland did not offer an entrepreneurial environment at all in those days. After graduating from secondary school, I attended University College Dublin, where I took a degree in commerce, studying under Professor George O'Brien, who was on the boards of the Central Bank and of Guinness and was the Dean of the Faculty, and Garrett FitzGerald. One of the things I regret now is that I didn't get as much from my university years as I could have. I wasn't a great student; I was never brave enough to approach the lecturers and get to know them.

Years later, though, I was at my third supermarket in Sutton, and I saw Professor O'Brien doing his shopping. I went over to him to introduce myself, as I knew he wouldn't remember me.

"What are you doing working in a grocery shop?", he asked.

I explained that it was my shop, my third in fact, and he exclaimed, "Isn't it interesting that one of my commerce students has actually gone into business?". Most of my classmates would have become teachers, accountants or civil servants.

Business education is infinitely better nowadays. In Ireland today, there are excellent colleges with a business focus, such as the Quinn Business School in UCD, the Smurfit School in Carysfort and the National Universities. I'm an adjunct professor for marketing in NUI in Galway. I believe that Dr Aidan Daly, who works in NUI Galway, is a particularly impressive example of an educator working in the area of business.

As soon as I finished college, I went off to France. At the time, my assumption was that I would follow my father into the hotel business, and I felt that France would be the place to go. Arriving back in France after a brief detour to Brussels, I got off at the first city after the border, Metz. Within five minutes, I had found a job in the *Buffet de la Gare* – the station restaurant! I worked that whole winter in France as a waiter and doing kitchen work, but the most interesting thing of all, to me, was how one could go into a shop, pick up a newspaper or magazine to have a look at, and then go and pay for it. At home, I told my father about self-service, and he said, "Well, if self-service is such a good idea, it could work with food. People don't always want to read, but they do always have to eat!". We had read about self-service food being sold in America, and one or two places had opened in Ireland as well. In Dublin, there was a place called H. Williams, for example. I remember visiting it at the time; the whole idea of customers picking up products and then paying for them was extraordinary. People had the idea that the public couldn't be trusted not to steal things, and there was also the notion that you were paying for a service, for someone to do something for you.

One of the things I regret now is that I didn't get as much
from my university years as I could have, and I didn't make
university as useful to me as it could have been.

My first personal involvement with the grocery business was with a firm called Lipton's, in London. In the training session for new employees, we were instructed to take as much money as we could. When the customer came to the counter, we were to try and sell them as much as possible. If a lady asked for half a pound of rashers, you'd have to put on 10 ounces, or offer her sausages as well. This approach was complete anathema to me, because I had learned from my father to try and make every customer a repeat customer.

I opened my first self-service grocery business in Dundalk in 1960 when I was 23, with a loan from the bank and my father as guarantor. At that point, it was called 'Quinn's Supermarket'. It was the first supermarket outside Dublin, which made it one of the pioneers of a profound change in business culture in Ireland at that time. It was a very big shop by the standards of the day, although now it would fit into the fruit and vegetable section of a modern Superquinn!

When I first opened, I really came up against the long-established culture of retail in Ireland. A well-to-do lady from the area came in, very kindly, to give a young man some business in his first shop. She introduced herself to me, and I tried to pass her a basket, but she said, "I'll have one of those and one of those …". We walked around the shop together as I put things into the basket for her and tried in vain to pass it to her so that she could do her own shopping. When we got to the till, the lady said, "You have my address, haven't you?", and I had to explain gently that we did not deliver, nor did we run a credit tab to be cleared at the end of the month, as she was used to. In an effort to explain to our customers what the self-service baskets were for, we put up a sign, "Please take a basket!". One day shortly after we opened, my father came for a visit. As he walked down the street, he saw a couple of people strolling around with our baskets. They had assumed that they were being given away for free, and had done exactly as the sign had suggested!

As the 1960s and 70s progressed, self-service became more and more important in Ireland. One of our counterparts was the Quinnsworth chain headed by John Quinn, who was really the Michael O'Leary of his day, growing his company quickly and advertising heavily. Because of the similarity in names, customers would get confused between us, so we changed our name to 'Superquinn' in 1970.

After the self-service revolution, one of the biggest changes in the retail industry was the introduction of barcodes. In 1974, I went to the annual convention of the Food Marketing Institute, and was shown a prototype of barcodes and scanning. I was really excited by the whole concept. At that time, shopkeepers still had to stick price labels on all their products, and checkout operators had to key in the price manually. In a big supermarket, that was a lot of work and, if you had to change the price for some reason, you had to get someone to tag everything all over again. In the late 1970s, I went to London, where the Article Number Association had started, and then got the Confederation of Irish Industry, which went on to become IBEC, to hold a dinner at the Burlington for the 20 biggest suppliers in Ireland. The Article Number Association and the Cash Register Society came along to put on a display and to explain what scanning was and how it worked. Someone selling a product who was able to put a barcode on it, registered with the Article Number Association, could have their items scanned, providing a lot of information to the vendor, and saving them a lot of money. If there was a need to change the price of something in a shop, you just changed the sign; no more labels! I became chairman of the Irish Barcodes Association in 1980 and remained so for 10 years. We didn't get into scanning until 1986, about a year after L&N, which introduced them for the first time in Cork. Later, we used barcodes to introduce Ireland's first loyalty card, the Superquinn club card. When the card is scanned, the customer's name goes up on the screen in front of the person on the checkout, who can then address them by name.

All these changes were huge for the retail industry, but alarming for the trade unions, which were concerned about the impact that the changes would have on all the people who had been employed to stick on labels, and because employees now just had to scan barcodes rather than ringing up prices. We brought the unions in to see how the system worked and to show them how it was more efficient.

The next big change was Internet shopping, which we introduced in 2000.

I had to delegate, and give work that I had previously done myself to other people. The curious thing I discovered was that, quite often, these other people were actually better at doing things than I had been myself.

Through all the changes, our focus was always on customer service. In Superquinn, we used the symbol of the boomerang for our approach. A boomerang always comes back, just as we wanted our customers to return. Newly-qualified trainers were given a little badge in the shape of a boomerang to wear; more recently, we made sure that everyone wears theirs turned so that it also resembles a smile.

Speaking personally, I always found paperwork very boring and always wanted to be on the shop-floor, so I found a good way to keep meetings as short as possible, which was to hold them standing up. We also developed the system of holding meetings early in the morning with no cup of coffee or breakfast until it was over, and by only meeting after everything that was agreed the last time had been done. For me, it's always been very important being on the shop floor and meeting people.

Our policy at Superquinn is that the manager's office should always be on the shop-floor, because the belief is that the manager shouldn't be sitting upstairs doing paperwork. If he's got paperwork to do, he can do it on the shop-floor. We have our managers' offices at the customer service desk, where the manager is constantly interrupted by customers, which I see as an advantage rather than a disadvantage.

I feel that I was lucky, because I got into the supermarket business at the right time. It would have been difficult trying to open a chain of supermarkets 10 or 15 years later, and 15 years earlier, it would have been impossible because there would have been no goods to put on the shelves then, as at that point products came in sacks and bulk packaging, and there'd have been no way to display them.

In Superquinn, we used the symbol of the boomerang for our approach. A boomerang always comes back, and we wanted our customers to return to us in the same way.

I have always been interested in joining trade associations around the world. One was the Food Marketing Institute, in Washington, D.C., and I joined the board in about 1989, and CIES, which is in Paris. I'm still on the board of both. One of the benefits of joining as an organisation and sending out people to conferences has been to network. At Superquinn, we attended conferences and met counterparts from other countries. We would also go and visit each other and learn from what other retailers were doing.

One that comes to mind was UKROPS in Richmond, Virginia. This was an organisation very much like ours, and when we met they had just gone into banking. They had tied up with a local bank, and introduced branches in all their shops. We arranged for them to come over and give us a hand and, together with TSB, we formed a new company called Tusa, the Irish for 'yourself', to serve as a bank. We had just opened the 14th branch when it became clear that, for many reasons, it just wasn't working out. What was particularly embarrassing was that, when we had launched Tusa, we had received such favourable publicity that people were queuing up to work there, and even leaving solid jobs in the banking industry. We had taken on about 100 people altogether when we realised that Tusa was losing money hand over fist, just a year and a half after starting. While, of course, we weren't happy about Tusa's failure, trying something new and accepting when it wasn't working was part of the business culture that we had created at Superquinn. Trying out something new that didn't work out was fine; the real failure was not even trying. We had developed a system of trying out new innovations in one shop to see how they would go before unrolling the idea elsewhere; Tusa had been the only exception to this rule.

Tusa was one of our more notable failures but, of course, we had our successes, too, including our in-house sausage-making facilities modelled on a supermarket with a sausage factory that I had visited in Nuremburg, which produced award-winning sausages, and our in-house bakeries, an idea borrowed from France's supermarket chain, Carréfour.

Visiting businesses overseas was always a rich source of inspiration. On a trip to Ottawa in 1983, I came across a supermarket selling bulk food, resulting in huge savings for them, and we started selling some items in bulk. We also introduced 'no label' products, again following the example of Carréfour. We launched our black-and-white packaged generic products, which came from Ireland, just before Quinnsworth unleashed its Yellow Pack items, which it imported from Canada.

Regardless of the environment, if you get up in the morning looking forward to going to work, you have a much better chance of succeeding.

I n 1984, I became chairman of An Post when the old Department of Post & Telegraphs split in two to become Telecom Éireann and An Post. For the supermarket, this meant learning to delegate, and it was a little humbling to realise that many employees did a better job without me looking over their shoulder. In fact, Superquinn started to perform better when I was busy elsewhere. At An Post, the big challenge was to instil in the staff the idea that it was OK to try something new, even if there was no guarantee that it would work. Previously, all the staff had been employed as civil servants, and were answerable to a Government Department. This meant that the postal service was not a very easy environment for innovation. The idea 'If it fails, it fails' was anathema and had to be fought.

Now, there was a bit of rivalry between Michael Smurfit and myself. He had just become chairman of Telecom Éireann; we had both been picked as non-political appointments. At the time, Telecom was being presented as the sexy side of the operation, the thing of the future. Telecom put huge banners around the country, and lots of ads on television saying, "We're sorting out the telephone system!". The 12,000 former civil servants who were now working in An Post almost felt like second-class citizens, so part of my job was to help them feel more enthusiastic and positive.

A colleague, Gerry Liston, came up with an idea: "Why don't you launch it with a penny post on the first day, so that everyone who writes a letter that day can send it for just one penny?". That was a great idea, but we couldn't tell anyone, even the employees, because of course the banks and so forth would hold back their post and send them all out on that day. So, we started out sending a lot of penny stamps to all the post offices in the country.

"This is not a good idea", people said. "The first thing Feargal is going to do is put the stamp up by a penny!"

I went on *The Late Late Show* that night and announced that, on Tuesday morning, everyone who had a handwritten letter to send to anyone in Ireland, including the Six Counties, could do so at their local post office. This was a huge boost for post offices, especially the small ones, which were often tucked at the back of a shop, because suddenly everyone wanted to send their letters. Four million stamps were sold at a penny each. Of course, it cost An Post a lot of money to post all these letters at a penny each, but the interesting thing was that all the elderly aunts and other relatives who had not received a letter in ages suddenly had letters that they felt they had to reply to, so a week after the penny stamp, there was a mini-boom in letters being sent back at full price!

In January, just around the same time, someone said, "Did you ever think of trying to get people to send St. Patrick's Day postcards to their friends all over the world?".

I thought that that was a good idea, so I proposed a selection of cards pre-stamped for postage. The post office people came back and said that they had figured out that, for 25 pence, we could afford to bring out a card that could be posted anywhere in the world.

"We'll definitely have a go", the guy in charge said, "and we'll get started straight away. We'll get tenders out to get the post cards made, and we should have them in by mid-March."

"What?", I asked, "but St. Patrick's Day is in March!".

"You didn't mean *this* year, did you?"

The old Civil Service way was always to get tenders, but we went to our advertising agent and asked him to get six artists to produce six designs – religious, humorous, patriotic, and so forth – and we had them within 48 hours. The cards were on sale in good time. We sold a million in the first week and then another million.

Between the success of the penny stamp and the success of the St. Patrick's Day card, people at the post office got a huge boost in morale and gained hugely in confidence, while the poor people at Telecom still had to wait for several years to get all the equipment they needed.

The following year, we tried to follow up these successes with the concept of persuading Americans to send their friends actual postcards 'from the old sod'. We did a big mail out to people with Irish names in the USA. We had worked out how much money we would make if 5%, 4% and so forth of the people sent a card. In the event, even less than 1% did, so the exercise cost us a fortune and was a huge failure. The former civil servant employees said that they would have "had their fingers cut off" when they had been answerable to a Minister. As Government employees, any failure would have been an embarrassment to the Government; as employees of a business, they could make innovations that, at times, might not work out.

*For me, it's always been important to keep the humour in
the workplace and to keep smiles on faces.*

Waking up every morning with lots of things to do, and being able to start new things and get a buzz from that is a constant source of motivation. So, in 1992, I decided to run for the Seanad, and was elected the following year. My way of dealing with the Seanad, of understanding how I could find a role in it, was to use my experience and look for the customer in each piece of legislation and then ask myself how we could improve the customer's experience. As soon as I found this approach, I realised that I could come up with things that might not occur to other people from different backgrounds. A few weeks after I was elected, the Unfair Dismissals legislation was coming through, under the then Minister, Mary O'Rourke. This would make dismissal on grounds of religion, gender, sexual orientation or for being a Traveller illegal. I looked at the legislation and thought about the customer and it occurred to me that age should be in there as well. I remembered someone on the board of a hotel that I had been involved with saying to the manager, "Can I make a suggestion? Would you not put a bright, young, attractive woman behind the reception desk? It's nice to walk into a hotel and see a good-looking woman and the one you have on there is a bit old and she's not very good-looking". The manager had better sense than to replace an excellent worker just because of her age, but I remembered the story and suggested adding age to the Unfair Dismissals bill. While there can be some difficulty in determining who belongs to the category "Traveller", for example, there is no equivocation about age. The law was passed with the amendment, and I was very pleased. Afterwards, two different trade unionists came up and told me that they were amazed, because they had studied that particular piece of legislation months before and had sent it out to the different branches, and nobody had thought of age. They were astounded that an employer could come up with such an idea.

*A successful business will be the one that recognises the
customer and manages to hold onto them,
even when times are difficult.*

S eeing a smile on customers' faces has always been a wonderful
motivation to me, in whatever area, from supermarkets to the
Seanad. Sometimes, when I'm in one of the supermarkets, and I
see someone who is clearly well over the legal drinking age with a
bottle of wine in their trolley, especially older ladies, I go up and say,
"I'm afraid we've got a problem with the wine. I'm afraid we need to
see proof of age". I think that my feeling that smiles on faces are so
important harks back to the Red Island days, when my father was
running the holiday business and it was all about making sure the
customers had a great time.

While I feel that the fundamentals of retail have always been the
same, and probably always will be, obviously there are changes in
culture that affect the way things are done. For one thing, the role of
trade unions today is different, and smaller, than it used to be. The
unions are not nearly as required as they were before, because I think
that good employers want to keep their employees and realise that
they have to work hard to attract and keep the best people, so union
membership has actually dropped dramatically, although of course,
there are individual cases when unions are very valuable. In times of
full employment, unions always struggle to hold onto people. It's a
different story when factories are closing and jobs are being lost; then
unions are important to fight for the people.

I am still president of Superquinn, but I no longer have any direct
management role in the organisation. When I stepped down in 2005, I
wondered what I would do with my time. My wife Margaret thought
maybe I would relax a bit, and maybe take care of the garden, but the
first thing I did was to become chairman of Eurocommerce, which is
based in Brussels, and represents all retail, all wholesale and all
international trade in Europe, trying to influence the Commission and
the Council of the European Union. I love doing the garden, but I
didn't like the idea of it being my main activity of the day.
Eurocommerce has been a fascinating experience.

I found a good way to keep meetings as short as possible,
which was to hold them standing up, meeting early in the
morning with no cup of coffee or breakfast until it was
over, and by only meeting after everything that was agreed
the last time had been done.

R ecently, someone said to me, "Business isn't what it used to be. It used to be so much more relaxed". I didn't remember being relaxed! Personally, I think that business has always been equally tough and difficult. I remember my father telling me how, in the 1950s, a friend of his would yearn for the good old days in business, while my grandfather, back in the 1930s, had used the exact same words to complain that, "It's like it was in the old days. It's very tough now!".

In tough economic times, some businesses will struggle to survive, and there's always the temptation to feel that, if a company is to succeed in recession, corners will have to be cut. That is usually a short-sighted approach and a sensible business will be the one that recognises its customers and manages to hold onto them, even when times are difficult. In fact, business is just as tough in good economic times, or tougher, because in that situation people are encouraged to go into business who maybe shouldn't.

Young people in Ireland today are in an excellent position to succeed in business. For one thing, they have a lot more experience of business, at least as consumers. They have seen customer service at first-hand. In America, in particular, friendly, efficient customer service is part of the culture, and I've seen how young Irish people in America quickly absorb what they need to do. In Ireland, in general, customer service is improving and becoming more American in style. It was very different for my generation; as young people, we didn't go out to restaurants, we didn't go to businesses and we didn't see people working who would give us an example of what we should be doing. Another important plus for young people is that the standard of education today is much higher in general than it was in my time, when most students left secondary school at 13 or 14. Most students in Ireland today pursue some form of higher education.

Changes in culture and technology inevitably bring changes in business. While the switch to self-service did mean that some sorts of business went under before, nowadays there are certainly categories of business that will not exist in the future, or at least have to make some very serious adaptations. This is not a bad thing; just one of the natural challenges that businesses face. When cars were invented, and carriage-makers started going out of business, the smart people thought, "I'm not just in the carriage business, I'm in the transport business," and they modified their trade. Businesses today have to do the same thing.

Those who go into a way of life they actually enjoy are the most likely to do a good job, and they will be the ones able to make the changes necessary to succeed. Regardless of the environment, if you get up in the morning looking forward to going to work, you have a much better chance of succeeding. If it gets to the point whereby it's no longer a joy, it's unlikely you'll do a good job. That's my advice: love what you do and you will do it well.

Successes and failures both gave us something to learn from.

12
NIALL QUINN

Niall Quinn is the chairman of Sunderland FC. He was born into a sporting family in Dublin in 1966. His father, Billy, played hurling for Tipperary. While playing all sports as a youngster, hurling was Niall's favourite and he went on to represent Dublin in an All Ireland minor hurling final in 1983.

Niall Quinn joined Arsenal in 1983 and went on to Manchester City and Sunderland, where he became a great favourite with the people in the North-East of England. Niall Quinn played soccer for Ireland, receiving 92 caps throughout his career. He retired as a player in 2002 and has returned to live in Ireland.

Subsequent to his career as a footballer, Quinn worked as a commentator on television and in the print media. He has also proved himself in the world of business, particularly in his chairmanship of Sunderland FC, a British club whose fortunes have seen a major positive turnaround since Quinn took the helm. When Sunderland was relegated from the Premiership in 2006, Niall put together a consortium of mainly Irish businessmen to buy the club. He secured former Manchester United captain, Roy Keane, as manager and, the following year, the team won the championship and gained promotion to the Premier League at its first attempt.

Niall has worked with a number of charities and contributed the entire proceeds of his testimonial to charities in Dublin and Sunderland. In 2003, he received the Beacon Fellowship prize for his contribution to children's and medical charities, as well as an honorary MBE, among many other awards.

Although he is professionally based in Sunderland, Niall and his family live in Co. Kildare, where both he and his children are deeply involved with sports at a local level.

A SCÉIL FHÉIN

I grew up in Perrystown in the parish of Crumlin, a working class area in the south of Dublin city. About half the people living there were indigenous Dubliners, and half were 'blow-ins – country families who had come to Dublin for work. My parents were from Tipperary originally, and I always have a lot of contact with our extended family in the country. In those days, of course, Crumlin seemed much further away than it does now: Tallaght in the south of Dublin was still just a big farm; now there are quarter of a million people living there.

My parents originally had emigrated to England, where my elder sister was born, but, when the rest of us started coming along, they came home, much as I would later on with my own children. Everyone on our street looked out for each other, and all the children played together, sometimes until as late as midnight, when the odd time the guards would turn up and send us off to bed. There was a real community feel in the area. I have to say that my childhood in the 1970s was as near to idyllic as it could possibly have been in the context of the economic hard times in Ireland in those days.

This was partly because two wages were coming into the house; my mother was a teacher and my father worked at Boland's Bakery. He had been a serious hurler for Tipperary in his day, playing on the county team until work brought him to England. When my parents came back to Ireland, he got involved again and played for Dublin in club hurling with Faughs and won a Dublin championship with his team. As a small child, I used to go sometimes to watch him train. My mother's brother, Niall, was also a hurler, as well as a high jumper, who jumped in all the big meets in Ireland. From both sides, I learned the important message that sport is about more than winning and losing. although I have to say that I got probably got a better balance more from my mother's side; my dad was always the lunatic with the hurley on the side of the pitch, roaring and screaming and questioning the referee's parentage.

From very early on, sport was my big love, and I played morning, noon and night on every sports team imaginable. I was on the table tennis team, the hurling team, football teams and soccer teams. One of my proudest memories still is of winning the Community Games *puc fada* all-Ireland long puck competition, under 12s, when I was nine, 10 and 12. In those days, Dubs weren't expected to win against the lads from places like Kilkenny and Tipperary – and some of them were three years older than me, too!

Throughout my childhood, I was so busy with sport, I didn't have one single free night in the week. That was a big worry for my mother, who was not happy about my not getting my homework done, and about the notes sent home from the school. I remember trying to do my homework one morning, as I was riding to school on a friend's bicycle crossbar.

My mother would have loved me to do my Leaving Cert and to go on to get proper university qualifications but the opportunity arose to play professional football and I jumped at it. Personally, I think she may have been better off, as I think I would have embarrassed her with my results had I stayed on in school.

My father took me to all the GAA club and county matches he could around the country. The GAA is hugely important on both sides of my parents' family, with players on each side having represented their county at hurling. When I was about eight, Dublin won the All Ireland football final, heralding what would be an amazing time to be growing up in Dublin with a team that used to beat Kerry every year.

I believe that helping children to understand the importance of team values is one of the most crucial things they can master; certainly, it was for me. Now, near our home in Co. Kildare, my daughter is on the county under-14 team, and my son plays soccer for Kill and Gaelic for Eadestown. Because of their involvement in sport, they are both beginning to realise just how important teamwork is. Whatever they end up doing in life, teamwork will certainly be part of it; it was, and still is, for me.

Towards the end of the 1970s, we got a colour television and sports on television started to become a feature of my life. *Match of the Day* on Saturday evening and *The Big Match* on Sunday morning got me hooked; I knew about every player in every club. I made it my business to know as much as I could. I wrote to football clubs looking for stickers and all the information I could get – not just with soccer, but with just about every sport.

*I'd always asked a lot of questions of people, no matter
what company I was in. I'd never been too shy about
finding out, trying to get into their psyche and see what
makes them sort of be that edge ahead. It could be any walk
of life, be it business, sport, whatever.*

From as far back as I can remember, I was heading towards a career in sport. At the very beginning of my life in football, I played for my local team, Manortown United. The manager during my seven years with the team was Ciaran Flaherty, who really helped me to learn how to believe in myself. The soccer teacher at secondary school, John Molloy, was also very important to me; he believed in me. He pushed me in the right direction and played me in the under-18 senior team in my second year, when I was only 13.

In my last year in Ireland, before going to play for Arsenal, I spent time playing with the Lourdes Celtic club. Now, that really toughened me up. There was a huge difference between this team and the one I'd played with for the previous seven years. It was an inner city team and was regarded as a top class club with a long tradition in producing talented players. The boys on the Lourdes team were tougher lads than the players at Manortown. I can remember once we had to pick a player up to play from the local Garda station, where he had spent the night! Unlike Manortown, these players were used to the pressure of schoolboy football at the top flight. I learned a lot about football and about how to mix with different types of people, which stood me in good stead when I went to London.

I went over to London to play on trial with Arsenal when I was 16, just a week after the All Ireland minor hurling final, which was the second week in September. I had played my last soccer match of the season in April, concentrated on hurling all summer, and squeezed in a month touring Australia as captain of the Dublin colleges Australian Rules mixed team. At this stage, I was planning a career in the GAA when, suddenly, an Arsenal scout knocked on the door. I was as fit as a fiddle, but I hadn't played soccer for months. Fortunately, the try-out went really well, so there I was, within a fortnight of having played in an All Ireland minor hurling final, now I had the offer of a three-year contract. I signed on 6 October 1983, my 17th birthday. That same week, I was offered a professional contract by two Aussie Rules clubs in Australia, to play Aussie Rules in Australia, but that seemed a long, long way to go for a 17-year-old. There was no Frank Stapleton or Dave O'Leary to mentor me there. Four weeks earlier, my big preoccupation had been the All Ireland minor final and in the aftermath, "Would I make the Dublin senior hurling team?". It was breathtaking stuff at 17.

I sometimes wonder how my life would have gone if I had accepted the offer for Australia instead. I'd like to think I would have acquitted myself quite well. Jim Stynes, who took up the contract instead of me, went on to become one of the most famous Aussie Rules players of all time. I'm not saying I would have done as well as him, but I like to think I could have had a good career in Australia. I will never know now!

The situation facing young footballers in the early 1980s was much less formal than it is today. I found myself in London, a huge smile on my face, walking into the dressing room and seeing men who had been football heroes of mine: Dave O'Leary, Pat Jennings and Charlie Nicholas. I was in cloud cuckoo land for the first year. If somebody kicked me, I was most likely to say, "Sorry. Is your foot OK?". I had some toughening up to do! Something that stood me in good stead from the very start was maintaining relationships with people outside the world of football. In the early years, a lot of my friends were Irish boys working on London's building sites. Football lent me a certain amount of glamour, but some of them were earning far more than I was and, when it came to needing a few quid on a Monday or a Tuesday, I was often the borrower rather than the lender. Keeping my feet on the ground and knowing that some of my friends had real problems to contend with helped me to keep issues like a bruised toe in perspective, even as the team was being brought to the best hotels in the British Isles, travelling overseas and being interviewed by television and the press. That's not to say I didn't find it all very exciting, because of course I did. When you're winning, a dressing room is the best adult playground in the world!

In those days, Arsenal was just coming out of the wilderness, and I was there for the start of it. I was with Arsenal when they won the

League Cup in 1986/7. For me, playing with Arsenal was a wonderful way to acquire an education in football. It is a proper football club. As young players, we were taught that discipline was crucial, and we didn't dare get sent off by a referee. In those days, the young players finished their football duties at two or three in the afternoon, and a bus would collect us and drop us all off at a snooker hall. It might sound strange, but I learned a lot about life from the characters I met at that snooker hall too and in the bookies and pubs as I had reached the inquisitive age of my late teens. Some of them were very odd, but I still appreciated them. By the time I was nearing the end of my teens, I started going out more with the senior players. I watched and learned and, while I was thrilled to be with them, I was careful not to be too wild. I didn't want to be the one to make a fool of myself in front of them!

In those pre-Celtic Tiger days, I used to travel home every few months and, on the way to Ireland, there would be just three or four people on the plane. On the return flight to London, the plane was always full. All the bright young people were just leaving in their droves, and I knew at least a dozen places in London where I could pop in for a drink and be sure of meeting people I knew from home. The IRA was still carrying out bombing campaigns in the United Kingdom and, of course, this affected how Irish people were seen there. On 17 December 1983, just after I signed with Arsenal, several people were killed when an IRA bomb exploded outside Harrods of Knightsbridge. I went into the snooker hall the next day, where they knew me well only to be told, "F... off Paddy, there's no snooker for you today".

At 23, I signed for Manchester City, which is where my career really got going, under Howard Kendall. I joined with eight games to go and we were bottom of the league. Luckily, I scored a few goals and started to get popular with the crowd, especially when those goals helped us to stay up. It was all another great adventure.

Around that time, in 1990, Ireland qualified for its first World Cup, and I scored the equaliser against the Netherlands, allowing us to pass into the second round, so it was a really important period for me. It didn't sink in just how important it all was for Ireland until we were flying back, and the pilot took us over O'Connell Street to show us all the people gathering for a parade in our honour. Looking down and seeing what seemed to be hundreds of thousands of ants all over the bridge and the streets around, it was the World Cup moment for me and a million times more memorable than any goal could ever have been. Four years later, the Irish team went to America for the next World Cup. I knew that most Americans don't care much about soccer, so it was astounding to see the Irish-Americans out in huge numbers, just to catch a glimpse of us. But things have changed for today's Irish team. I hope that Irish people today know how difficult it is going to be for Trappatoni to recreate that sort of feeling. The whole culture of football has changed, and along with it the sort of joy and pride that people used to feel in the national team. Just recently, I read that Ireland's good performance in the 1990 World Cup played an important role in kick-starting the whole Celtic Tiger phenomenon; what a contrast with the way the Irish team was in the last couple of years.

> *The greatest thing I learnt in that time is that it is so important is to be able to look ahead. Looking back is fine, but tomorrow is what life is all about.*

After *Italia 1990*, I returned to Manchester and became the first person since Brian Kidd in the late 1960s to score 20 top-flight goals for Man City. Nobody has done it since. I was on a complete high, and, at one stage, the evening papers reported that AC Milan was hunting me. Back then, the Italian league was the best in world football, with the English league trailing far behind. Then the Premiership came into being and the rest is history. All this was all happening to me just a few years after I had been playing in Croke Park as a minor hurler, so it would have been easy for all the excitement to go to my head. Thankfully, I coped with it by hanging around with people who helped me to keep things in perspective. Football, and all the attention it brings, can consume people. I did do the snooker halls, the gambling, the drinking and all the rest of it, but I survived it. Possibly because I had grown up as a teacher's son, I had enough discipline to know when I'd reached my limit and when I needed to stay at home and rest. I regret the amounts of money I used to gamble away, the late nights but, most of all, I regret the friends of mine who couldn't stop.

But I don't regret the experience of meeting the characters I did and the fun we had. In a strange way, it stood to me.

Second only to the experience of the 1990 World Cup in this period was a match in which I played for Ireland in a European championship qualifying match against England at Wembley. My family was very patriotic, so this was a really big thing for me. We didn't win the game, but I scored an equalising goal, and a photo of me running down the pitch just afterwards with "Ireland 1, England 1, Quinn" on the scoreboard is one of the very few pieces of memorabilia that I keep in the house.

A few years after signing up with Man City, I got a cruciate injury, which meant that my whole career was in jeopardy; many players never come back from that sort of physical damage. When new management came in, they weren't sure that they wanted to keep me and I was told that I could look for another club. I very nearly went to play for Sporting Lisbon, and even got as far as agreeing terms with them before the deal went wrong. For a while, I didn't play a great deal, and then the opportunity came up to play for a club in Selengor, Kuala Lumpur, and my wife Gillian and I went over. Things were difficult in England, because people thought that the fact that I had had a cruciate injury meant that I wasn't up for much any more. I came very close to signing for Selengor, which would have meant giving up the opportunity to play for Ireland's national team again, and also signalling the last chapter of my career, which was something I didn't really feel ready for.

Gillian, who was pregnant at the time, was not very happy at the thought of life in Malaysia, and fortunately, at the last minute, my old manager from Manchester City, Peter Reid, called me up and asked me to come to Sunderland, where he was now in charge. While there was much less money on offer than the Kuala Lumpur position would have offered, this was a great break.

Unfortunately the joy did not last. During my fifth game for Sunderland, I ruptured my other cruciate. The future looked bleak. Even with the advances in medicine, players are told that they must not play for seven or eight months after such an injury but my career was at stake. I played a Premier League derby against rivals Newcastle four-and-a-half months after the operation. It was extreme, but I needed to do it to convince the Sunderland people. I just had to get out on the pitch, since I'd got off to such a bad start. People had seen me come with one gammy knee and now I had another! I had to work very hard to get fit enough to play well and win back their support, and I take great pride that I was able to turn the situation around. Apparently, the people who recover best from cruciate injuries are short and stocky. I was the exact opposite and I had to fight even harder. I read somewhere that liver was good for you, so I ate it morning, noon and night, and I kept going to the gym to get myself back in shape. I was determined to keep looking forward and to focus on the next game. I was to enjoy five very exciting years as a player after that time.

As the end of my career as a professional player started to draw near, each event become more precious and important to me, and I got more and more focused. Twice, I arrived at the training ground and looked in the back seat of the car, only to see my two children sitting there looking back at me – I was supposed to have dropped them off at school 30 miles earlier. The girls who provided the players' food had to take care of them those days because I couldn't be late for training, and I had to ask them not to tell their mother what had happened! Several other days, I was so lost in thought that I missed my exit from the motorway and didn't even notice until I had gone far away from where I should be.

There were difficult times in those years too. After eight years as Sunderland manager, Peter Reid was let go, which affected me badly. I became grumpy and fed up and started to suspect that every offer had an angle. I realised that I was letting myself get into a bad place and I had to get out of it. I was lucky, because reaching the end of a career as a player is a very difficult time, not just financially but even more so in terms of the blow to esteem that the ego receives, and a lot of former players really struggle. The greatest thing I learnt in that time is that it is so important is to be able to look ahead. Looking back is fine, but tomorrow is what life is all about.

At times, it is good to reminisce and I suppose there had been a sort of wonder and joy in Ireland about what the Irish team had been able to achieve in 1988 and 1990, and nobody cared that the manager was English. There was just this great, innocent pride in seeing the green shirt doing well. The culture of sport has changed a lot in Ireland since and now there's a demand to have a definitive answer to every conceivable question, which is driven, in part, by the media. That innocent joy is certainly a thing of the past. Maybe the 2002 World Cup and the well-documented problems the team had with the departure of Roy Keane, its captain, has played a part. But you know the only solution is always to look forward. Right now, Roy is doing a terrific job as manager of our club and all the opinion, the negativity, the blame and everything else from that time does not matter now. Sport wins.

Go out there with a smile on your face.
This is what you're on this earth for.

T he 2002 World Cup was the last time I played international football for Ireland. It was tough to walk away but I had my head held high after 16 fairytale years.

My career as a professional footballer finished three months later at Sunderland and left me with years of fantastic memories. Goals come and go but, when I remember the good times, I really have to recognise how privileged I've been. The funny thing is that I remember very little about the matches I played in. Most hardened professionals remember every detail, but what I mostly recall is the fun after the match. I remember the dressing room scene following each good victory I was involved in. I simply blacked out the defeats, and went straight on to the next match. That's something I learned as a child: "OK, we may have lost the football match last night, but I've got a hurling match on Tuesday, and we're going to win that". If I had been interested in nothing but soccer from an early age, maybe I would have been more driven. People have told me that the game would have meant more to me, but I don't think that I was any less committed than anybody else; I was always just able to focus on the future and the next game.

I didn't have the same nerves and built-up tension before a match as other players but, all the same, the need to know that everything was in good shape, physically and psychologically was always there. I was committed, 100 per cent. I did all the things I shouldn't have done to make games. I hid injuries. I had cortisone injected all over the place: shoulders, knees and ankles. I would pay for it later, which is why cortisone is banned now.

I'm happy that I made the most of my career, and I'm happy that I didn't get wrapped up in myself, because there's more to life than that. But I'm also happy that I made Man City's and Sunderland's *Teams of the Century* and that I made an impact. My whole career was played out at the end of an era in football. I think, for example, I was one of the last players to be able to crack jokes with referees during the game. I was on first-name terms with them all and, while I fell out with one or two, there were also times when I swapped my jersey with the referee at the end of an international match. Nowadays, if anyone saw that, they'd be looking to see if the match was fixed!

Today, the players are like film stars. Every match has about 80 cameras watching it, with two or three on each player. After the match, it's even worse. When I was a young player, we could go to an ordinary pub for a drink and, while people would come up to us, they didn't see us as being that different to themselves. I see myself as fortunate, because I don't think that today's generation of young footballers are having nearly as much fun. They are wrapped in cotton wool most of the time and taken care of in every way and, as a result, when they do go for a good night out, they often end up getting into trouble. They have money, but they haven't had the chance to really live. I see them at Sunderland FC, of which I am now chairman. The young trainees that come into football are better protected now. They are guaranteed their place in college and we insist they acquire academic qualifications should things not work out. We have purpose-built classrooms where they study and tutors to help them learn. They are chauffeur-driven most places they need to go; there is nothing left to chance. Personally, I would not have enjoyed that sort of treatment, and I doubt that I would have been able to develop my spirit of adventure. I would also have missed out on a lot of learning experiences found in unexpected places: late night card-playing in snooker halls, gambling, the drinking debates in back street pubs and all the rest of it.

There are players who had good agents and accountants who skilfully moved them from club to club. This makes the modern player lots of money and they can rightly say football was good to them. But football was great to me, because my mind is full of wonderful memories that have nothing to do with money and success. From my very first day at Arsenal, and right through my subsequent periods in Manchester and Sunderland, I had a smile on my face and a passion for the game. I might not have been the greatest player, but I was one who was able to maximise the experience, to get the most I could from it. It was always an adventure. Now, as a father, I try to help my kids see challenges as adventures rather than reasons to feel nervous or upset. When they have a big match coming up, I tell them to go out with a smile on their face, and to let their thoughts propel them to the next level. The fact is, in sport, when you are enjoying yourself, you do well, and when you don't enjoy yourself, flaws start to appear in your performance – it's as simple as that.

I'm fascinated by sports psychology, and especially the 'we' side of it. The sport that I was brought up in was all about teamwork with the emphasis on 'us' not 'me'. I admire people who can get teams to gel together, make them work as one and to get them to understand the importance of what each brings to the team.

I'm no sports psychologist but, when you are enjoy yourself, you perform well, and, when you don't enjoy yourself, flaws start to appear in your performance – it's as simple as that.

A ll the years I lived in England, I never stopped feeling a sense of giddiness when the plane start to get close to Dublin and the pilot said, "Put your seat belts on. We're landing in ten minutes". I had always stayed in touch with what was going on in the GAA scene in Ireland. I regularly attend GAA matches and I haven't missed a match involving the Dubs for years.

When I finally did come home with my family at the age of 37, we all got to know everyone in the village where we settled immediately, because I joined the local football team and my son and daughter did too. It is a marvellous way to repatriate. I'm delighted that my children are into sports, because learning about teamwork will be an invaluable lesson for them, whatever they eventually decide to do but, to tell the truth, I'm not so sure I'd like my son to become a professional footballer. Why? Because I think it's no longer possible to enjoy the football world the way I did. For me, it is far more difficult now. The culture has just changed too much. Expectations are too high for young players. From day one, they cannot put a foot wrong. The reality tells us that seven out of 10 players do not make it. And while I admit it's a sheltered life and that today's players are totally cocooned from the real world, it is not always a positive thing. But if he does wish to go down that route and he shows the ability, the will and determination to succeed, then I will support him every inch of the way. Given the opportunity, every parent would do the same.

After winding up my career as a footballer, I had planned to have a nice easy life, doing a little bit of television and playing golf every day. That was impossible, I just couldn't do it. I now realise I am driven and need a quest. Towards the end of my career, I had worried a little about all the money that I had wasted, and wished that I had listened more to the advice I received when I was 18 – but who really thinks about planning sensibly when they are 18? In any case, I had started a pension back then, which was good, and I had been lucky with a purchase of land that I had made with my World Cup money, back in 1990 when land was cheap. In sport, I'd never been shy in trying to find out what makes people have the edge and what keeps them ahead of the rest. There are many people I admire outside of sport too, great business people who have led their teams to the summit.

In 2006, I got together a consortium of Irish business people to take over Sunderland FC. I know Sunderland well, and there are many similarities between the sports culture in the North-East of England and the GAA culture in Ireland. The Sunderland culture still has the sort of friendliness that has become a little bit lost in parts of Ireland. By that I mean Sunderland has not been affected by any Celtic Tiger and reminds me very much of the Ireland I grew up in. There are still big similarities, for instance, when Sunderland plays Newcastle, the passion and excitement is a lot like a Dublin v Kerry encounter back home.

Sunderland FC was huge in pre-war days but, when we took it over, despite having good infrastructure, it had been in the doldrums for a long time. Our job was, and remains, to turn that around and get Sunderland to join the big boys again.

The Drumaville Consortium is composed of self-made individuals with huge, very different talents. As chairman of the club, my job has been to get them to believe in it. As a businessman, I have had to learn a lot very quickly and, as a fellow who never did the Leaving Cert, I still have a lot to learn about corporate governance. I have never worked this hard in my life before. I look at the various people in this group, how they are self-made and how they worked their way to the top. They are an inspiration and have been hugely supportive of the whole process and they retain huge ambition for success for the future.

My background as a football player has been invaluable to me in this new venture in more ways than one. Because I worked for newspapers for a while – *The Guardian* in England and the *Irish Independent* at home – as well as having done television for Sky, I understand how the media works, and how media people see the industry. I also understand the culture of the dressing room and what goes on in players' minds. Now I'm on the side of ownership and governance, so I'm rounding off my education in the industry. While I haven't racked up a lot of experience as a chairman of other companies, I would see that as a good thing rather than a weakness. Some great business people, such as Alan Sugar, have come into the industry from other areas and haven't been able to make it work, because they just don't understand the various football functions.

I live in Ireland and commute to Sunderland. Early on in this role, I had to spend six days a week over there, coming home on Saturday night and heading back early on Monday morning. Now I've got better at delegation and have made good strides towards having the system that I need in place. I spend Wednesday, Thursday and Friday working, Saturday is game day and, wherever we are in England playing, I try and get a flight home back late Saturday night so that I can spend at least Sunday, and usually Monday and Tuesday, with my family. When we have midweek football, I need to be over more often. My office is at the stadium and I have a fantastic personal assistant who holds everything together. I've had to become very efficient with Blackberries, emails and other things that don't usually exercise a footballer's mind!

Sunderland has been very welcoming to me and to the other Irish people involved with the club. A lot of the pubs in Sunderland have adopted Irish names. At the same time, a lot of Irish people are interested in Sunderland. We have over 1,000 Irish season ticket holders, and there are flights coming in every week full of Irish fans to attend matches. One thing about the English is that they are very inclined to be accommodating when people have something to bring to the table. The Irish are very different to the English, and add a lot to the sporting world over there, from horses to football.

> *I don't know enough to give people advice about products*
> *or about sales technique – I'd be a big picture person.*
> *But, whatever you're in, you'll be successful if you are six*
> *months ahead of everyone about you.*

I find inspiration for work and business primarily in the men nearest me in the consortium, but there's also a lot of inspiration to be found in the sporting world. One person whom I've always admired hugely is Mohammed Ali. When you look back at his early television interviews, you can see how that young man, at just 19 or 20 years of age, was able to hold the greats of television in the palm of his hand.

Specifically, in terms of taking over Sunderland FC, one person in particular was enormously helpful, and that was Denis Brosnan of the Kerry Group. Although he is not involved in the consortium, he provided me with structure and a way forward. Basically, I turned up and his doorstep and said, "I want to buy a football club!". "I think you're mad," he said, "but if you do it this way, you have a chance". When Denis speaks, I listen to every word, because he is the sort of person who has vision and who is also procedurally correct in the way he approaches things. Denis helped me to look at what we needed to do with Sunderland FC and to divide the task ahead into four steps, outlining how we could achieve each one. Because of him, when I was sitting in front of potential investors, I managed to look as though I knew what I was talking about! Thanks, Denis.

To succeed in sports management, it's crucial to have a passion for the sport, and an understanding of it, even if you haven't been involved in the sport as a professional player. For instance, I think I could probably manage a hurling team. I haven't played much since I was 17, but I've always watched the game, and I've always returned to Dublin to go to matches. Since childhood, I have loved the GAA, and one of the things that I appreciate about it most is its purity, because the players are amateurs. They do it for the parish or the club or the county rather than for money, and it's a wonderful contrast to the cynical professional dressing room where all the talk is about the agents and what they are getting for the deals. On the other hand, if I was asked to manage a hockey team, I'd make a mess of it, because the passion and the knowledge of the game just aren't there. The same goes for succeeding in any industry; the passion has to be there.

As a sports person in the commercial environment, I have had to be prepared to hold my hand up and say, "I don't know a lot about this. I've got to learn fast. I've got to listen. I've got to take things, good or bad". Most importantly, I need to be able to assume authority without looking like I think I know it all, because of course I don't. The trick is to stay open to being educated all the time, while at the same time appearing to know what you are talking about.

> *The most important thing is to assume authority*
> *but not try and make it look like you're a know-all,*
> *because we all learn.*

So far as leadership goes, sport has taught me a lot. I like to start with teamwork. At Sunderland FC, I found a lot of very talented employees who had been left downtrodden by all the negativity in the place. The club was going down the pan and most of them hated coming into work every day and were being prevented from growing within their roles. I knew that I had to turn that atmosphere around, not just with the players and but also with all the other employees of the organisation, amounting to 120 non-playing full-time staff. They all had to have a reason to come into work, champing at the bit and happy to be there.

Our PR people, for example, had inherited a situation in which they had to ban people from the stadium if they dared to write anything bad about the club. There was an awful atmosphere between the media and our PR camp. It had to change. I told them, "Hey, I'm not here to do your job. You're in charge of PR. Go and court the media again. It doesn't matter if they have been writing bad things because, when we turn this club around, they will be writing great things about us. They have to say it as they see it." Soon the press liked what Roy and I were doing.

The importance of giving people space and positioning them well is something I really learned in my football days. Look at the Ireland team in 1990: if Jack Charlton had played Paul McGrath left wing, or Packie Bonner right side of midfield, we wouldn't have had the success we had. Good management is about putting people in the right places and letting them express themselves. In football, a manager can build spirit and passion but he can't move the players' legs. It's the same in business.

I have read that just 20% of all workers love coming to work, with another 20% actively hating it, and the other 60% arranged along the spectrum in between. For most, their boss sets the atmosphere in their place of work and determines how they feel about it. Just like with kids playing football, having a smile on your face means you'll work well. I want to make sure that the employees of Sunderland FC are among the 20% that loves coming to work.

A football club is a complex organisation. At Sunderland, for example, we have a conference and banqueting group with a lovely facility where we do weddings, funerals, bar mitzvahs and so on. We take in the guts of £4 million a year with liquor sales and all the rest of it, so that is very important. We have lots of sponsorship, from main club sponsorship to advertising boards and jerseys. We have boxes that we sell each year, with a dedicated sales team just for that division. We have to work hard to maintain momentum and stay on top of being ready for what is coming down the line. A lack of structure in the first place was why Sunderland had got into a bad position.

For instance, the new players whom Roy and I have signed in the last couple of years have very different contracts to the players who were signed previously, insofar as players are now rewarded for doing well in the form of bonuses on top of their basic wage. Before, players were paid the same, regardless of how well they did, or did not, play. Also, every one of our players' wages will be halved if Sunderland is relegated. Unlike before, this safety net will protect the club into the future. Naturally, relegation is a development we desperately need to avoid. It would ruin our momentum and make it very difficult to bounce back. And it would be devastating to Sunderland's supporters.

I think that, more than in most industries, in sports we have to be mentally in the future, seeing where the industry is going, and being able to prepare for where the club will be in a year or two. I am not in a position to advise business people about product or sales technique, but I do believe that the businessperson who is reading the industry six months ahead of everybody else is going to succeed. So far, at Sunderland, I can see what's coming and what's possible, and the dream that I was able to sell to investors was a future in which Sunderland was in the Premier League. Remember that when I was trying to convince these people the club was a laughing stock, relegated and on its knees – but I knew the potential. I was able to show that potential to the investors, to show them the structure that we were going to use, and to talk about how we would make it back to the premiership. So far, so good!

Over the next five years, we have to really kick on and attempt to make Sunderland a top Premiership team. This is something that is already beginning to happen. Already, our average crowds are enormous; the fifth largest in the English league, bigger than Chelsea, for example. We find ourselves in the Premiership for a second year, and we have to use this consolidation to get better and better – and, who knows, we could end up mixing with the big boys in Europe!

We have huge ambitions for a team that's won just one trophy since the 1930s. That's important for many reasons, and one of those reasons is simply that the rest of our business cannot prosper unless the players are going out there and winning games for us. One difference between a football club and other types of professional organisations is that no matter how skilled the board is or the manager or nine-tenths of the workforce are, it all rests on the players on the field. So much rests on how the players perform because, without good performances, our product just isn't there and none of the ancillaries sell. We sell, when the team wins. A lot can change if the team plays badly, or if the referee makes a bad decision at the end of the game. That means that all our employees are biting their fingers every Saturday when the team plays and the result is completely beyond their control.

The commitment was there. I was driven, and I'm happy that I made the most of it. But I'm also happy that I didn't get wrapped up in myself. You know, there's more to life.

I thought, when I retired from playing professionally, that I might take it easy and relax a bit, and while I do relax with the kids, have a few pints every now and then, and even go to Nashville once in a while, there's plenty of work left in me still. I still have the desire that everything I do, I should do wholeheartedly and I still have the desire to win. I don't want to turn up for a charity golf tournament, play badly and dismiss it with, "Oh, I didn't have a great day". No, I want to win.

I'm lucky because, although I am not still playing professionally, I am doing something that I had a love for as a kid, and a passion for and I didn't have to go to college for years and years, hoping to get a break, it happened within a week! I am still very much on the trail that I started out on as a child playing for Manortown United. I keep saying that, one day, I'll slow down, but that's not going to happen. I wouldn't last more than two or three days. Sunderland still has a lot to achieve, and I still have so much more to learn about business.

Besides, after joining my local GAA club, Eadestown, and at the age of 40, we won a Kildare Junior county championship by a point after extra time. That night, going to sleep, I was just as thrilled as I ever was by any victory.

And I still think there's another county title, or maybe even two, left in me.

Football was great to me, because I have great memories. I've got a mind full of great moments that were nothing to do with money, that were nothing to do with scoring goals. They were to do with what it's all about. And I'll take them with me forever.

13

JAMES SHEEHAN

In 1984, James Sheehan established the Blackrock Clinic, a private clinic, where he was a specialist in replacement hip and knee joints. He is Director of Blackrock Medical Partners and he was also instrumental in the development of the Galway and the Hermitage Clinics.

James Sheehan graduated from UCD in 1963 and went on to become an orthopaedic surgeon in St Vincent's Hospital and Cappagh Orthopaedic Hospital. He was awarded the following medals in clinical examinations and in his final medical examinations: the McArdle gold medal in Surgery, UCD; the Feeney gold medal in Obstetrics, Coombe Hospital; the Bellingham gold medal in Medicine, St Vincent's Hospital and the O'Ferrall gold medal in Surgery, St Vincent's Hospital.

Mr Sheehan is a Fellow of the Royal College of Surgeons of Ireland and holds an MSc in Bio-engineering and a PhD in Mechanical Engineering from the University of Surrey. He is a Fellow of The Institution of Engineers of Ireland and of the Irish Academy of Engineering.

James Sheehan is widely recognised as having transformed the face of private healthcare in Ireland, and is hugely respected as a businessman as well as a medical professional. A strong proponent of the value of an independent hospital system to complement State healthcare, he has been a prominent objector to the Government's proposed co-location system for hospitals.

A SCÉIL FHÉIN

I was brought up in Dublin, but was born in Kerry in 1939 and spent the first two weeks of my life there, so I can claim to be a Kerryman when the occasion demands! I attended St. Mary's Holy Ghost school in Rathmines and went straight from there, at the age of 16, to University College Dublin to study medicine, after sitting my Leaving Cert. There were five of us in my family, and four went into medicine, although neither of our parents worked in this area; my father was in the office at the Dublin Port & Docks Board. In those days, the late 1950s, students could do whatever they wanted when they left school with a basic Leaving Cert.

On getting into UCD, I was very aware that my parents were under pressure to put us all through college, even though things weren't difficult at home. The fact was that there were four of us in third level education at the same time. This was one of the reasons why I was so committed to what I was doing. I worked extremely hard in pre-med and was amazed when, at the end of the year, I came in first place with first class honours. That gave me a huge boost to continue working hard, and I was very driven from then on. I put every effort into what I was doing, and I maintained a burning desire to get into medicine.

I graduated in 1963, did an intern practice and then went into surgical training, initially in St. Vincent's Hospital and then in Cappagh Hospital. After that, I moved to the UK for a time, working first in Glasgow, then in London, in the Royal National Orthopaedic Hospital and later with Sir John Charnley in Wrightington Hospital.

Sir John designed the first artificial hip joint, the Charnley hip prosthesis. During my time with him, I became very interested in the design of implants. He had a workshop where I trained with a lathe and milling machines, producing spare parts. At that time, all the artificial joints that we put in were finished on the premises. While the polishing and hand-finishing was not carried out by the surgeons, we all trained in the workshop in aspects of the metallurgical production. Sir John's first successful joint was inserted in the early 1960s; now this is one of the most common procedures carried out around the world. At the time when I met him, anyone who wanted to use artificial joints had to work with him for a period or, at least, visit and spend some time in his unit. This was a very exciting time for me, and had a big impact on my attitude towards medicine.

My experience with Sir John Charnley and his implant programme interested me in engineering and, realising that I didn't know enough about it and that all orthopaedics is based on stresses and engineering principles, I returned to university to study bio-engineering at the University of Surrey, and went on to do a PhD in mechanical engineering over a seven-year period. My interest in engineering was purely with a view to progressing in surgery. After finishing my training and studies in England, I returned to Ireland and took up a consultant's position at the new St. Vincent's Hospital, which had just opened. In 1970, I set up the joint replacement unit in Cappagh Hospital, with a small research workshop and the first sterile-air operating theatre in the country. Now, Cappagh has the second largest joint replacement unit in Ireland and Britain. I worked in Vincent's and Cappagh for 17 years. When I started working as a surgeon, we still saw a lot of health problems that just aren't seen anymore. Much of what we did in the early years of my career is now obsolete and, in fact, the whole spectrum of disease has changed within that cycle of my lifetime of practice.

I and two colleagues knew that a third of the population was covered by private insurance, and thought that we could set up a hospital where we could do work on that group of the population and free up the public system.

I n the early 1980s, there were huge cutbacks in government spending. The Department of Health decided in their wisdom that they would save money on medical expenditure, and chose artificial joints as an area where money could be saved, because costs were easy to identify. This limited the number of operations we could carry out to just two a fortnight, which left me with very little to do. Now there was a five-year waiting list for people who needed artificial joints. I had two colleagues who were both in similar positions: one in nuclear medicine, where there was no expenditure on new technology, and another in cardiac surgery. We knew that a third of the population was covered by private insurance, and thought that we could set up a hospital where we could do work on that group of the population and free up the public system. Until then, all our private work had been done in public hospitals, because most of the private hospitals didn't have any facilities for high-tech work. Mount Carmel had been the only private institution where I could do joint replacement. There was only one unit in the country, the Mater Public, where heart surgery could be carried out and, if a private patient was brought in, someone on the public list was displaced. For all these reasons, we decided to set up Blackrock Clinic.

I had never studied business and had no business expertise at all. Then, as now, I was driven by patient care and the quality of patient care. So far as I saw it, business was a necessary evil to make progress in these areas. I believe that, in healthcare, business is commonsense. If patients are taken care of properly, and the business makes any degree of profit at all, I would see it as successful, because the main aim of being in business in medicine is to look after patients and ensure a good outcome for them whenever possible. My aim in business is to look after our patients as best we can, while making enough money to propagate the organisation. I suppose that this is quite different to what a lot of other people might consider a business ethic.

I bought the site for Blackrock in 1981, just when the recession of the 1980s was reaching its peak. I had to mortgage my own home to finance it. Banks like personal guarantees, because they know that people who are totally exposed just have to make it work. Initially, we developed a consultant block, which was separate from the hospital. We sold the consulting rooms on to various doctors and, when we had enough activity on-site, BUPA came in as a partner with us and we built the hospital. All of that took a few years. Back in the 1980s, interest rates were running at an average of 23%. Today, people complain when interest rates rise from 2% to 4%! Throughout the building of Blackrock, we were paying 23%.

*My aim in business is to look after our patients as best we can,
while making enough money to propagate the organisation.
I suppose that this is quite different to what a lot of other
people might consider a business ethic.*

I retired from surgery at 63, having been asked shortly before to look at facilities in the West of Ireland because, at that time, a lot of the medical services were very poorly developed. There was no radiotherapy for cancer care, for example, and cancer services generally were in disarray. There was no cardiac surgery. I was approached to see if it would be possible to replicate the Blackrock Clinic in the West of Ireland. Initially, I wasn't very interested. I thought that I didn't need that sort of stress at that point in my life. After some pressure, I gave in and said that I would consider it on the basis of setting up a community hospital in the West of Ireland.

While business can be very exciting, there are aspects of it that I don't enjoy. In the area of healthcare, in particular, there's the tendency for people to point fingers and say, "Oh, he's just in it for the money!". Certainly, people said that about me with reference to Blackrock. Nothing could have been further from the truth. I wanted people to get a better quality of care than that available in Ireland at the time and I had to put my own home on the line for that to happen. I was very committed to the project. I wanted a community hospital that was owned by the community, so I set up and registered a charity called 'The Galway Clinic Limited'. I appointed a fundraiser in Galway who worked for me for a year. After a year, we hadn't raised a single euro. Nobody wanted to subscribe to a charitable hospital.

In the meantime, I had assumed that we would be able to raise the money, so I had had plans drawn up by architects, struggled with the planners because the site for the hospital was designated for agricultural use and, together with my brother who was also involved in the project, spent a considerable amount of my own money. We submitted plans for rezoning the site, which were rejected by the council by one vote. At that point, having spent about €500,000, I decided that I didn't want to have any more to do with the project if this was going to be the attitude in the West of Ireland. Later, the mayor and some of the council asked me to reconsider, and I very reluctantly resubmitted an application because they assured me that they would fast-track the application through the council. The application was passed, by a majority, and things got started. We were still committed to doing it on a charitable basis, but we hadn't raised any funds.

By now, the building was two stories high and the banks wouldn't lend us any more, so the site was closed up for six months. Of course, at that stage, the media was interested when we locked up the site! Larry Goodman, who has been a close friend for 25 years, rang me up and said, "I see you're having difficulty in Galway. Is there anything I can do to help?". He offered to come on board on the basis that we would convert it into a business model, and that he would invest in the project. With these changes, I was able to renegotiate with another bank, Anglo Irish Bank, which is an extraordinarily satisfactory group to work with. The Galway Clinic opened its doors in 2004.

On completion, Larry Goodman and his associate, Brendan McDonald, became involved as 50% shareholders. We had borrowed €100 million and, while we raised a lot of money from the doctors who bought their consulting suites here, we are still carrying debts to the tune of €50 million.

For me, public work is the ultimate aim of the community hospital. I would like to see 50% of our beds occupied by public patients. That would be the ideal community mix in it, and if I see this achieved, I will have accomplished my goals.

During the process of trying to raise funds, I had approached Charlie McCreevy, who was then Minister for Finance, to see if he might structure a tax-based scheme for hospitals. Similar systems were already in place for car-parks, houses and university residences. McCreevy did introduce a Finance Act in 2001, which extended tax advantages to investors in private hospitals. These advantages apply only to investors who put in money for 10 years and, overall, it reduced our original capital cost by about 10%, which is a help but doesn't make a huge difference to a business's success or failure. There is no tax break for developers, despite what a lot of people think!

Also in my dealings with Charlie McCreevy, one of the things that I pressed to have introduced to the Finance Bill was that public patients should have access to independent hospitals. We would designate 20% of our beds for public patients, and the State would finance their treatment. I wanted to avoid some of the problems that had emerged in Blackrock because it had been labelled as an elite hospital, which was far from our intention on setting it up. There was a significant Labour element in government prior to the opening of Blackrock Clinic, and they felt that it was a fancy private hospital, rather than a high-tech institution for people who couldn't get the care they needed in the public sector. As a result, they insisted on the VHI introducing high-cost plans for so-called elitist hospitals. This made it very difficult for those without such plans to access treatment, as they had to pay a considerable premium themselves. Having failed to establish the Galway Clinic as a charity, I felt that the next best thing would be to have it as a community hospital available for everyone and that, if the Finance Bill stipulated that we were obliged to designate 20% of our care to public patients, hopefully the State would start funding people going to private hospitals. At this time, the concept of treatment purchase funds were being evaluated; these are funds set up for public patients who were waiting for elective surgery for more than three months. Currently, nearly 20% of our beds are dedicated to public work and, for me, public work is the ultimate aim of the community hospital. I would have liked to see 50% of our beds occupied by public patients. I would hope that, in the future, we will see hospitals like ours treating 50% of the public patients and 50% of insured. To me, that would be the ideal community mix in it, and if I see this achieved, I will have accomplished my goals.

At the Blackrock and Galway clinics, we pride ourselves on keeping our staff numbers very low. We automate everything we can, and maintain an obsession with crucial things such as hygiene. We emphasise the comfort and safety of the clinic environment. I feel strongly that, when people are sick, that they are entitled to as nice as environment as if they went to a hotel. Why should hospitals be seen as a poor relative? Hospitals often have been run down and not nearly as clean as they should be. I believe that all sick people, public and private alike, are entitled to a much better environment than what has been available to them in the past.

Traditionally in Ireland, consultants work in both private and public medicine. Because there is such a great need for consultant services here, we are trying to attract people to our staff in the Galway Clinic who are not also involved in the public sector. We guarantee our new consultants an income for a limited period of a year or two, because many are coming from abroad, and this is a very difficult thing to do with no job security. As they get established, they pay us back. This system enables us to find and work with really great people. For example, in Galway, we have two young surgeons who graduated in Ireland and acquired experience in Australia. They are trained in robotic surgery, and Galway Clinic offers the only robotic programme in the country for prostate cancer. These are all services that could be made available to public patients if the State would pay for them to be treated here, and our hope is that this will become possible by means of the treatment purchase fund.

My interest in healthcare lies in complementing what does and doesn't happen in the public system, not to compete with it.

D espite a certain amount of progress in recent years, many of the interactions I have had with State bodies have been enormously frustrating. My interest in healthcare lies in complementing what does and doesn't happen in the public system, not to compete with it. The idea is that if something is missing we can provide it. After setting up the Galway Clinic, I started trying to get in touch with relevant senior figures in the then Western Health Board to see how we could work together to provide comprehensive healthcare to the people of the West of Ireland. I finally managed to speak to someone weeks after my first attempt to make contact. I was told that they didn't want to meet me or know anything about what I was doing because my work could take from their budget and interfere with their scene. That's what passes for co-operation from the State sector!

Over the years, we've managed to build a slightly better level of co-operation, but I am still baffled why the University Hospital in Galway averages between 15 to 20 patients on trolleys every night when we send them an email every day telling them how many empty beds there are in the Galway Clinic. They could easily transfer patients with private insurance to our facilities, at no cost to themselves, and make more beds available to people in the public system. You could count on one hand the number of patients referred in the last four years, because the State system would rather pretend that the independent sector doesn't exist. In that respect, the business of healthcare has changed very little as compared to 20 years ago.

There is still an immense divide between State-run services and the independent services, which the State does its best to ignore. For instance, in planning radiotherapy services for Ireland, State authorities have completely disregarded what is happening in the independent sector. The State has been informed that it needs a certain number of radiotherapy units to treat our population, when in fact there are quite a lot of facilities in the independent sector that are ready to take public patients, and are currently grossly under-utilised. We started radiotherapy when it wasn't even available in the public system, and we introduced radiotherapy to the West of Ireland. Ours was the first radiotherapy unit outside the Mater Private. Yet, despite the expertise and facilities we have in this area, the State prefers to act as if these did not exist. Here in the West, people ill with cancer were waiting for weeks to go to St. Luke's hospital for radiotherapy, when they could have been funded by the State to attend the Galway Clinic with no delay. In fact, the Galway clinic treated eight patients with very advanced cancer who were too sick to travel to Dublin for free, because the State would not fund their treatment in the independent sector. If they were still alive, a few months down the road, they would get treatment in St. Luke's, but they could not avail of treatment near their home. This was a real shock to me, because I had always assumed that, if services were made available by the independent sector, the State would use them. I cannot understand why the public and independent sectors cannot co-operate; it doesn't make sense on any level. Similarly, cardiac surgery is available at the Galway Clinic, and I feel that we have sufficient capacity to deal with all the cardiac patients in the Western region. Two years after we opened our cardiac unit, the State duplicated it at vast expense. Neither of our services is operating at anything near capacity. We could have saved the taxpayer the many millions spent on building and equipping the State-run cardiac unit.

Healthcare is a very sensitive area because our customers – patients – are in a very vulnerable condition. Anyone who is sick is anxious and apprehensive and there are inevitably family concerns and worries. Running a hospital entails a lot more than just running a business. In fact, if a healthcare facility is run purely as a business, it is doomed to fail, and administrators of healthcare facilities do need to understand the field. When I initially went to Scotland after graduating, all of the hospitals there were administered by doctors. This was a system that worked very well, because their understanding of the institution was very different to that of a pure business administrator. One of the problems that hospitals and clinics grapple with is the divide between doctors and administrators. Often, administrators will go home at five o'clock, while doctors might find themselves working all night struggling with inadequate equipment.

Irish bureaucracy and policies cause huge problems for businesses, and medicine is no exception.

D espite the constant challenge of running our organisations, in the private sector, we are much more efficient than the public sector, largely because the levels of bureaucracy are so much tighter. For example, the Galway Clinic was built in 18 months, and commissioned in 19 days. The same builder was contracted at the same time to build a State hospital in Tullamore, which remains unopened, and the Galway Clinic is now in its fifth year of operation. The public system wastes an astonishing amount of public money, and there could be huge savings if it was better organised. Currently, there are 12 new operating theatres in St. Vincent's Hospital that remain unused.

The public sector talks about accountability, but has not yet got around to designing hospitals for the equipment that will be put into them, because it waits until hospitals are nearly completed before going to tender for the appropriate equipment, and then rebuilds them for the equipment to go in. They move so slowly that, by the time hospitals have been built and commissioned, equipment is obsolete! If we in the independent sector can build and commission a hospital in a year and a half, there's no reason why this should be impossible in the public sector. Irish bureaucracy and policies cause huge problems for businesses, and medicine is no exception. In the medical area, we have to pay VAT on everything, but we can't claim it back because medicine is not a VATable activity. This means that we donate a 21% surcharge to the government on every piece of equipment that we buy. There are no concessions for rates. The tax breaks that are available are now so diluted and require so much administration and organisation that they are often not even worth availing of.

Of course, a certain amount of regulation is important in any sector, and healthcare is no exception. I would like to see the government's main role in healthcare to be setting regulatory standards. Currently, we have no licensing for private hospitals, which can be opened by anybody, and we have no Irish system of accreditation. Independent hospitals in Ireland today have to go to an American accreditation board, the Joint Accreditation International. Their requirements are extremely demanding and detailed, and there's a need to have a specification and a protocol for every single thing, with only the highest of standards. Not one single public hospital would qualify for accreditation according to these standards. The HSE overcomes this by setting its own regulatory standards and licensing its own hospitals. At the same time, we are in danger of becoming grossly over-regulated in a lot of areas.

Fortunately, the graduates that we have found to work with us at our clinics are very highly qualified, and we are lucky to have an extraordinary group of people who have done medicine and who are very motivated. In general, however, I would feel that our national education system leaves quite a lot to be desired, in terms of creating both healthcare and business professionals. This is a problem that is going to continue to be a challenge in Ireland for the foreseeable future. In medicine, for example, there is the issue of the fact that 70%

of our emerging doctors are now women, because girls tend to be more successful in the Leaving Cert. This isn't sexual equality, and it isn't good for Ireland! We do need 50% of the entrants into medicine to be male, because when all these women doctors start having families, there will be gaps in the healthcare provided to the Irish public as a result of doctors taking maternity leave, career breaks and working part-time. We also do not produce nearly enough doctors in this country in general. We have a need for an additional 2,000 consultants, who simply are not available, and going to countries like India and Pakistan and depleting them of medical professionals who are urgently needed there is not a viable solution.

One of the problems that we are facing in Ireland is the fact that our education system has seriously failed to keep up with the times. In medicine, not only have we failed to qualify nearly enough people for our requirements, but we still need most of our graduates to go abroad and acquire additional expertise in other countries. We need people to come back to Ireland and introduce their new ideas to our system. This isn't true just of medicine; the same applies in every profession. The points system, which is so central to the Irish education system, is an utter disaster, because half the young people leaving secondary schools do not get to study their first choice; that's daft. The points system is not an indication at all of the individual's ability to perform in later life. Many people, including a lot of boys, often mature after a few years out of school, and are capable of achieving a lot more than their exam points indicate.

People working independently in healthcare will always do well if their patients are satisfied with the calibre of treatment they receive. I don't see why medical professionals should have an automatic right to a livelihood from the State, and I firmly believe that they should all be self-employed and feel a constant need to keep patients satisfied. I feel that this would lead to better professional standards in medicine, and I think that hiring doctors as State employees and guaranteeing them an income, regardless of their performance, is wrong. We honestly only need a tiny number of State employees in medicine, such as certain core psychiatric services. The same goes for other professions. In law, for example, apart from specific areas where we need legal advice from the State, I feel that lawyers should be self-employed. When people have to make their own livelihood, the levels of motivation will be high. The very concept of a State contract for life is utterly wrong. It breeds laziness. We have many wonderful people of the highest calibre working in State positions, but we also have a huge amount of inefficiency. Nobody should be a State employee for life and given a God-given right to an income and a pension for their lifetime without having to make sure that standards are maintained.

We don't need to do sales and marketing at the Blackrock and Galway Clinics, because this is done for us by satisfied patients. In the end, that is all you need to run a successful healthcare business; quality of service. That is something that has never changed. The healthcare provider that does its job well will never be short of work to do!

People working independently in healthcare will always do well if their patients are satisfied with the calibre of treatment they receive. We don't need to do sales and marketing at the Blackrock and Galway Clinics, because this is done for us by satisfied patients. In the end, that is all you need to run a successful healthcare business; quality of service.

PART 2

YOU CAN DO IT, TOO!

Apply yourself.
Get all the education you can, but then,
by God, do something!
Don't just stand there, make something happen.
It isn't easy, but if you keep your nose to the grindstone
and work at it, it's amazing how, in a free society,
you can become as great as you want to be.
And, of course, also be grateful for
whatever blessings God bestows on you.

Lee Iacocca,
former President of the Ford Corporation
and the man who became President of Chrysler
and saved it from certain bankruptcy

14

GRAB YOUR OWN OYSTER!

The interview subjects in Part I have given us a unique insight into their lives, both business and personal. I have endeavoured to portray their personalities, with some investigation into their formative years, their approach to life and the primary driving forces of their individual success. This has taken the shape of each of our entrepreneurs telling us their own story. The stories were written after extensive background research, in-depth interviews and, in many cases, interviews with friends and colleagues. In most cases, the research entailed a number of interviews, lasting many hours. The time spent by our contributors during the formative and primary research for this project, and their openness in divulging information, has made possible this entire book.

It was a more difficult process than I originally anticipated, as I was dealing with a diverse group of people who had achieved substantial success in their individual fields. A brief sample of the awards held by our contributors are given below, to highlight the calibre of the people who gave of their time to ensure that this project is a success. This list has been compiled to illustrate the esteem our entrepreneurs are held in by their peers and their industries and to highlight their professional standing.

In no particular order, some of our subjects have been honoured with the following prestigious awards: *People of the Year*; Ernst & Young *Entrepreneur of the Year*; JCI Ireland *Entrepreneur of the Year*; honorary knighthood; Papal knighthood; honorary doctorates; membership of Seanad Éireann; *Retail Excellence* award winner; Beacon Fellowship prize winner; past president of the SIMI; and adjunct professorships.

Their individual influence in the field of business is enormous; I estimate that, collectively, they have had a hand in the employment of over 75,000 people. The financial contribution from their endeavours to the socio-economic fabric of our country is in itself colossal. By any measurement, our entrepreneurs have been immensely successful. As people and individuals, they have all displayed certain characteristics that define entrepreneurial success.

This part of the book attempts to understand what it is that makes people successful in business. The following chapters have been assimilated from the wealth of knowledge and information uncovered in our interviews. I hope that when you have read it that you will have achieved two goals:

- You will have gotten to know our subjects a little better and will understand that background, educational achievement or institutional influences have little influence in the success of a determined entrepreneur.

- You will understand a little more of the requirements for success and, hopefully, will be better prepared to establish for yourself a more conducive personal space which I hope will enable you to succeed in your chosen field.

What is outlined in the following chapters is my interpretation of what is required for entrepreneurial success. It is solely a matter of opinion. This opinion is formulated from my interaction with the subjects of this book. Their experience and expertise has illuminated for me many of the points outlined in this section. It is not intended to be a definitive list, rather its aim is to provide a starting point for anybody looking to commence a commercial project or simply to indulge in a little personal development.

It is a guide and, while I acknowledge that this section in itself will not guarantee success, it should considerably enhance your chances of success if you adopt and use the principles contained herein.

15

TWENTY DEFINING CHARACTERISTICS OF SUCCESSFUL PEOPLE

H aving character is usually taken to mean that a person is honourable, honest, reliable, truthful and responsible. In short, that a person has integrity. This is true to an extent but it does not go far enough, as this definition outlines only what characteristics are required to be a good and balanced person.

This is as true for our business personalities as it is for ourselves. The business leader must have honesty and integrity in dealing with his or her workers and customers. The same is true for reliability and other forms of character. The leader must be ethical and conscientious in all activities. The character of a business reflects the character of its leader.

However, the entrepreneur will display another set of characteristics that define them as being an entrepreneurial person. It is a set of attributes that enables them to see an opportunity, to foster and nurture an idea or thought and to develop that thought into a viable business. These attributes are often regarded as some indefinable or intangible quality, one that is built into the psychology of the individual. They are perceived as a natural gift, one that cannot be learnt.

This could not be more wrong. All of our successful entrepreneurs readily admit to being average people with no special gifts or attributes. What they do exhibit is a determination and a willingness to try something, to work at it and to work on and develop their personal skills. They all demonstrate one ability: the capacity to learn how to get better. The characteristics of successful people are all learnt processes, not a preordained quality that somehow depends on our genetic makeup.

Our successful entrepreneurs are not unique, they are not especially gifted but they **are** special. They are special because they have made themselves special. They have worked on their skills. I believe that all of the core skills exhibited by our entrepreneurs are learnt disciplines. There is no secret to their success. It involves developing certain skills and a lot of hard work.

Below are the characteristics that all of our successful entrepreneurs have exhibited to some degree. This list is not exhaustive and none of the points are exclusive to successful or established entrepreneurs. Conversely, successful people do not necessarily have to display any, or all, of these characteristics. However, in my experience, it is highly unlikely that people will display much commercial success without displaying at least some of the attributes that have defined all of our interview subjects. The characteristics are:

- Attitude.
- Imagination
- Unwavering focus.
- Grace under pressure.
- Energy.
- Ability / capability.
- Opportunism.
- Pragmatism.
- People-people.
- Accountability.
- Work-life balance.
- Resilient.
- Goal-orientation.
- Effective communication.
- Strategic awareness.
- Sales-focussed.
- Service excellence.
- Natural-born marketers.
- Healthy relationship with money.
- Fire in the belly.

These characteristics certainly provide food for thought for any would-be entrepreneur. I believe they provide an excellent yardstick by which to evaluate your personal position *vis-á-vis* preparing yourself to succeed in business. If you do not believe you can mirror at least some of the traits outlined below, then perhaps it is time for some concerted critical self-evaluation.

1: ATTITUDE

This seems to be the number one attribute of any successful entrepreneur. Whatever obstacles may come down the line, they maintain a focussed, positive attitude.

It is interesting to note that, among the entrepreneurs interviewed for this book, their closest colleagues, personal assistants and senior managers all exhibited the same positive characteristic. In essence, these successful entrepreneurs surrounded themselves with positive, focussed, energetic people – people like themselves.

I strongly believe that, if there is one must-have characteristic for an entrepreneur, attitude is that characteristic – as evidenced over and over again by our entrepreneurs – so much so that the next chapter is devoted to it alone.

2: IMAGINATION

Imagine what it is you want to achieve. Imagine what it would be like to achieve it. Imagine what the rewards are. Taste it, feel it, enjoy it – because you need to understand what your mission is.

Imagination is the driving force behind progress. Everybody has one: some try to suppress it; others ignore its importance and its value in their personal development; most people are happy to indulge in fantasies or to imagine successful scenarios but they fail to act on their imagined goals – they do not answer the call to action.

Successful people not only display an imagination – they have acted on their thoughts.

Imagination is more important than knowledge. Albert Einstein

The entrepreneurs interviewed all exhibited an ability to visualise where they wanted to be, and what it would be like to be there. Whenever or wherever they saw an opportunity, they would always 'begin with the end in mind'. They imagined the goal and the actual situation that would result when they realised these goals.

This is a never-ending process as, once a certain goal is realised, the goalposts move and the process starts once again. Denis Desmond articulates this perfectly when he refers to the buzz he gets after a successful concert. There is an adrenalin rush when such a project is successful, perhaps even some celebration and then, the next morning, the realisation sets in that another concert or gig is imminent and the team must focus on achieving this success all over again. That's showbusiness for you – but it's reality, too!

3: UNWAVERING FOCUS

The successful entrepreneurs I interviewed were all completely focussed on the job at hand. When they were at work, the job and the people involved got their undivided attention – nothing else.

Some of our entrepreneurs said that, if you are committed to the success of a project, you have to live with it. According to Liam Griffin:

> *There is no nine to five in building a business. You must live with the business, foster it, nurture it and basically treat it as you would your family.*

All of our entrepreneurs demonstrated a willingness to stick with the project at hand, to focus on it as a goal to the exception of all else.

4: GRACE UNDER PRESSURE

An ability to thrive under pressure, without becoming stressed, is a key attribute of our entrepreneurs. They manage pressure and most certainly do not let it develop to the point that it becomes 'stress' in the medically-negative sense of the term.

Stress is an unavoidable consequence of life and, especially, of business life. Stress was identified in this sense by Hans Selye, who noted that:

> *... without stress, there would be no life.*

Successful people are able to manage stress and to turn it to their advantage, by turning it into an energy that keeps them focussed. They are able to achieve this focus, because they are able to relax and understand the importance of relaxation. This is not work-life balance in the conventional sense, rather it is their ability to enjoy their work. They love what they are doing.

Denis Desmond absolutely loves his job, promoting some of the biggest names in world entertainment. It is implicitly understood in his world that some promotions may not be a financial success and that the pressures that come with large-scale productions are part of the job. He has conditioned himself to enjoy the whole package, including the difficult times. Hence he does not 'do stress', but he most certainly thrives under pressure. This, I believe, is the crucial difference between stress and pressure.

5: ENERGY

The entrepreneurs were all energetic individuals and all physically fit. By maintaining a physical fitness regime, they were able to enhance their mental fitness and stamina for their respective business. Likewise, they all displayed an awareness that what they ate had an effect on their personal energies and abilities. In short, they all kept fit and had reasonably good diets. This, in turn, helped them to devote their energies to the projects at hand. It is also important in enabling them to handle stress, as discussed above. As I see it, physical fitness and an ability to manage stress are inextricably linked.

Energy for your business and life can be developed so easily. All it requires is for you to follow three simple steps:

- Watch your diet. Cut out, or cut down, on all fatty foods, caffeine, alcohol, etc. Eat healthily most of the time.
- Get enough sleep.
- Walk outdoors for 30 to 40 minutes at a brisk pace, three or four days a week. (Golf does not count, as it has little impact on cardio-vascular fitness.) A brisk walk regularly every second day will increase your cardio-vascular fitness and enhance your energy levels for everything, including work!

6: ABILITY / CAPABILITY

The entrepreneurs all exhibited an ability or capability to deal with a variety of different issues. But when I tried to understand what this ability or capability was, I found that it is many things and manifests itself differently in each of our subjects.

Ability in the sense of entrepreneurial ability is difficult to define. It can include the ability to cope, to communicate, to lead, to organise, or just common-sense, capability, reliability, social confidence, attitude – the list is endless, you take your pick.

Write down your own definition of ability / capability and compare yourself to it. Then make a list of what you feel you need to do to enhance this elusive characteristic in yourself. Then act on the list! A list is nothing but a collection of words, unless you take action.

7: OPPORTUNISM

Good luck exists and, equally, bad luck exists. Life is a lottery and, generally, the luck ratios will balance out for everyone. What makes successful people different is their determination to search for an opportunity or a lucky break and their ability to recognise it when they find it. It appears to be linked to attitude. The cynic will never recognise a golden opportunity, while the positive entrepreneur will see opportunity in every walk of life.

You may never find a four-leafed clover. Use a three-leafed clover and make it lucky.
Anon.

Our entrepreneurs are able to recognise and exploit an opportunity. So why is everybody not able to take advantage of the same situation? Presumably, because they think about it but never act on the idea. In other words, most people never work on their ideas. Thomas Edison probably summed it up best, when he said:

> *Opportunity is missed by most people because it is dressed in overalls and looks like work.*

8: PRAGMATISM

Pragmatism often required our subjects to be ruthless in dealing with problem situations. Ruthless in the sense that, if a business or department was not working efficiently and it needed remedial action, then remedial action was taken – immediately. If this required closing the business or laying off people, then so be it. The business came first and any individual stakeholder was seen as secondary. The rule was to take action – positive action, perhaps drastic action – and then move on and do business.

9: PEOPLE–PEOPLE

Our entrepreneurs are all people-people. They can empathise with and understand the other person's point of view. Hence, they are good team leaders and have a human resource within their business that is better than average and that they can rely on.

Every one of our entrepreneurs has built a team around themselves that is highly efficient, competent and reliable. Our entrepreneurs are demanding: they demand the same dedication and commitment to the cause from their staff that they exhibit themselves. They are meticulous and do not suffer fools gladly. They recognise that they rely on their core team and therefore expect unwavering commitment from their team. They can be quite ruthless in their search for the perfect team but will show great loyalty to their team once it is in place. In short, they recognise the value of good employees.

Anyone setting out in business would do well to adopt this approach. Always hire the best, never accept second best and work on building a team that you can rely on.

An ability to recognise competence in people and to attract it can be developed. Once good employees are in place, then their individual and collective achievements should be recognised. Our entrepreneurs all spoke about the importance of their team and the emphasis they place on developing the team dynamic.

In addition, the realisation that business is all about people, not products or services, is at the heart of the commercial approach of all of our successful business personalities. Irrespective of the levels of technological innovation or mechanisation in any business, the process always comes back to the concept of one person or group making a personal conscious decision to purchase goods, products or services from another. Like it or not, there are people behind every commercial act. It is essential that a successful businessperson recognises the importance of dealing with people and develops a person-to-person approach to all their dealings.

Our entrepreneurs all display a special ability to recognise the customer as a person. They can do this, because they themselves are customers. So are you. Each of you buys an immense array of goods and services every year. You enjoy good services and products and feel betrayed by bad service or poor quality products.

This is the ethos that lies at the essence of customer service. Put simply, our entrepreneurs always try to ensure that a customer's expectations are exceeded in some way. Exceeding expectations as a policy has emerged time again during the research for this book.

10: ACCOUNTABILITY

They also have courage in spades – especially the courage to take responsibility. They never pass the buck. This is because they realise that, no matter what, the buck stops with them. They have ultimate responsibility; they are accountable for everything that happens in the business. As Pat McDonagh AKA 'Supermac' puts it:

Nothing focuses the mind like accountability.

Every one of our entrepreneurs overtly and openly acknowledges that they hold ultimate responsibility for what happens in their organisations, good and bad. Padraig Ó Céidigh recognised this responsibility when he pointed out that, in business, since you aim to avail of the trappings of success, so also you should be prepared to accept the downside when things go wrong.

11: WORK–LIFE BALANCE

All of our entrepreneurs displayed a refreshing ability to achieve a reasonable work-life balance. They all have differing interests. They are all interested in their work. They are interested in their people but they ensure that they make time to be interested in themselves and their families. They all know how to switch off.

At Pragmatica, in our management and strategy seminars, we emphasise the importance of down-time. It does not really matter what floats your boat: holidays, fishing, golf, hill-walking, horse-riding or, indeed, floating an actual boat – it is essential to take time out to recharge the batteries. This is personal time and personal space and is essential to the mental and physical health of everybody.

Notice that all the examples I have used are fresh air activities. This is important as, in our increasingly sedentary lifestyles, we do not get enough exercise or fresh air. I never complete a seminar on development without emphasising the importance of a brisk 45-minute walk every second day. If undertaken regularly, this alone will bring about amazing changes in your life after only six weeks or so, as your health, energy and entire life force is enhanced by the exercise.

Likewise, with family, every one of our entrepreneurs highlighted the importance of making time for family. Take the time to be with them: your family are good for the spirit and can really put things into perspective. Once-important issues are very quickly put in their place in the order of priorities.

Feargal Quinn tells an amusing story of his passion for horse riding. He named his horse 'Business', so that whenever someone called looking for him when he was indulging in his hobby, his wife or secretary could answer honestly "He is out on Business!".

12: RESILIENCE

Failure is a fact of life. All of our entrepreneurs have made mistakes; some of them have made huge mistakes. What they have in common is that they all seen the mistake, taken note of it, drawn a line in the sand and moved on. None of them dwelt on failure but, equally, neither did they hide from it or ignore it. They recognised it for what it is: a fact of life. Then it is shelved, and they move on to achieve their goals.

Don't take setback personally: our entrepreneurs certainly don't. As they say in the best Mafia movies, 'It's just business'. If our entrepreneurs took setbacks personally, they would have given up long ago – but, as we have seen, entrepreneurs just never seem to give up.

Resilience is certainly a defining characteristic of entrepreneurs.

13: GOAL-ORIENTATION

Getting something done is an accomplishment; getting something done right is an achievement. Successful people, and most especially our entrepreneurs, are all goal-oriented, just as a successful sales person will always be target-driven.

One of the things that is different about our entrepreneurs is that they all have clearly-defined and documented goals. They write down their goals on an ongoing basis and review them regularly. They strive to achieve them and plan in detail the process to do so.

The crucial point to remember from setting goals is that it is essential to **write them down**. Unless a goal is written down, it's not a goal – merely a wish.

All goals must be **SMART**.

S - **Specific:** You must be precise about what you are trying to achieve.

M - **Measurable:** You must quantify your objectives.

A - **Achievable:** Are you attempting too much?

R - **Realistic:** Do you have the resources to make the goal happen?

T - **Timed:** State when you will achieve the objective: for example, by February 2010.

In successfully setting goals, you should endeavour to ensure that your goals are personal to you. Of course, they may involve another person or persons (after all, you can't do everything yourself) but they must be **your** goals, devised by you for you. They must be positive and involve some sort of affirming action. They must enable you to achieve your personal aims in a positive sense or fashion.

The final point to note about our entrepreneurs' goal-setting is that it is all in the here-and-now. The goal is always written in the present tense, in the now – not at some indefinable future date. Putting a time deadline on their goals ensures they are real time goals not some vague aspiration in the future.

14: EFFECTIVE COMMUNICATION

During the research for this book, each of our entrepreneurs was able to articulate their stories in a clear concise and succinct fashion. They were all interesting subjects and told their stories with humour and effect. They had a charisma that made the research an interesting educational and highly enjoyable experience. Each of our entrepreneurs is an excellent communicator.

Were they born with this skill? Does it come naturally? Well, it probably comes naturally now – but only after much work and practice.

Communication ability is a developed skill, but its importance to success cannot be understated. A clear confident communicator is always more likely to achieve what they wish, simply because they are able to ask for it in the best fashion. After undertaking this project, I have no doubt that we can all benefit enormously from developing our communications skills. We should never consider the development of our communication abilities as having an end; it is an ongoing process that requires continuous work.

Our entrepreneurs all readily admit to being better communicators now than when they started out in business. Why? Because they have worked at it and, while practice might not make perfect, it certainly makes better!

Who could forget the eloquence and passion of Liam Griffin in his media interviews after he managed Wexford to win the All Ireland final in 1996? His belief, commitment and passion were clear for all to see, but the moving eloquence with which such passionate feelings were conveyed was the result of many years of practice and developing his communication skills. As a public speaker, he has few peers.

15: STRATEGIC AWARENESS

Although all of our interview subjects had a plan, which logged their goals, aspirations and ultimate commercial destination, curiously they were less clear on how this was going to happen. There was an element of winging it, let's start on the journey and we will deal with the issues as they arise. Whilst they all had a plan, they were less rigid in the realisation of the plan. They implicitly understood that they could not pre-empt every problem so, in a way, they decided not to pre-empt any problem: they would just deal with them as they arise. Certainly, they examined the financial fundamentals but gave only a passing emphasis to operational problems, which would be dealt with in due course.

Anne Heraty put it clearly when she said:

It's not really about the job you are going for today, it's about where that's going to take you in three or five or ten years' time.

16: SALES-FOCUSSED

Contrary to popular opinion, selling skills can be learnt. The skills required for successful selling are not part of a person's character: selling skills are an acquired ability. They can be learnt, although it does take time, practice and application.

All of our entrepreneurs have developed this skill. They have recognised the importance of developing their sales ability or focus. Even if you do not believe you will be part of the sales team, you will have to be able to sell: to sell your concept, your abilities, your business' potential or your product or service – it's all the same, you will need to get other people to adopt your point of view.

Our entrepreneurs have all developed this ability, which is an essential skill for commercial success.

Our subjects all analysed each opportunity from the same general perspective. They all asked the same general type of questions when approaching the sales process, maybe in a different order or style but the content and end result are the same. They know they should know the answers. If they don't know them, they go find them – because they know that the answers are the key to winning sales. Our entrepreneurs all realise that successful selling in any environment requires a process-driven approach.

In each of our interviews, the selling process incorporated the following points, which are the cornerstones of developing a strategic sales focus:

- Who is the decision-maker?
- What is the value to the customer?
- What is the timing of the purchase?
- What is the effect on the sale of organisational or staff change?
- What external environment or events could affect the sale?
- Who are the competition? What do we know about them and what can we learn about them?

17: SERVICE EXCELLENCE

All of our entrepreneurs place a heavy emphasis on getting things right first time. They focus on development within their organisation and, most importantly, within themselves. They emphasise that the demands of customers are getting continually greater and, as such, they must always be working on their service, product and its delivery. The customer's experience is of crucial importance to the long-term health of the business. This is a point that comes to the fore, time and time again, in some shape or form, and is constantly emphasised as being of paramount importance.

For the purposes of this book, I have examined the entrepreneurs' definitions of service excellence or service quality and have found seven consistent threads common to all of our subjects' opinions on how a culture of service excellence is fostered and developed:

- Staff must support fully the drive for service excellence and continuous improvement. If customer service standards are to be integrated into the business with any hope of buy-in from staff, then the staff must be engaged in the process of development.

- Sense must prevail and all key personnel must be pragmatists in that they are willing and open to recognise limiting or poor standards of service or approach. They must also be willing to take immediate corrective or remedial action. The SWOT or gap analysis model is still valid for most commercial organisations. These are outlined later in the book and merit careful consideration.

- Development and transparency of customer service is paramount to success, as it is imperative that a transparent culture of service excellence is developed from the start.

- Consistency across the business. Inconsistencies of customer service delivery can occur within an organisation. Too often, customer service quality can fluctuate between outlets, branches or offices, and this can create real challenges in maintaining a reputation for excellence.

- Sustainability after the initial 'buzz' derived from the implementation. Service excellence must be sustained and developed over the long term. This is identified by our entrepreneurs as being the most demanding task in the development of a customer service culture.

- Regular monitoring and accurate measurement of performance. Feargal Quinn monitors his standards of customer service on an ongoing basis; in fact, his business model was developed to accommodate the continued drive to improve the customer's experience when in his supermarkets.

- Continual training and emphasis on service excellence as a concept. Pat McDonagh has outlined how the drive to satisfy his customers needs is never finished, as the bar is always getting higher, and hence we must never take our foot off the pedal. This applies to every person within an organisation and requires a continued investment in training and a consistent emphasis on motivating and monitoring the entire organisation on an ongoing basis. Padraig Ó Céidigh believes that, in the drive for service quality, "When it comes to service quality, it's the journey not the destination that counts, the job is never done …".

18: NATURAL-BORN MARKETEERS

All of our entrepreneurs have enjoyed tremendous success in their respective fields. They are all excellent marketeers and possess immense marketing ability and market awareness. They have all studied their markets, they know their product or service intimately and, crucially, they have evaluated where their product or service lies in the marketplace.

Let me clarify here and now that there is a huge difference between marketing and sales. Our subjects all alluded to this fact. Both marketing and sales functions are immensely important to the success of an organisation. Most organisations need to develop a successful sales function, since sales are the lifeblood of any business. But selling, whilst crucially important, is a functional discipline. It is a vital part of the overall dynamic but the overall dynamic will never exist without initial competent market awareness. An excellent sales person will flounder if they are pitching to the wrong market or if they are not properly directed. Marketing and market analysis is not more important than sales, it simply precedes sales.

The entrepreneur does not have to be a good sales person; such skills of course are desirable but they are not essential, since sales expertise can be hired if needed. However, any successful entrepreneur **must** be an adept marketer, otherwise they will not understand how their market operates and, by association, they cannot know how to position their business.

The good news for any aspiring entrepreneurs is that there is absolutely no secret to developing good marketing skills. It is a learnt discipline, which each individual will modify to meet their particular needs and the requirements of their specific market. It does require planning: a coherent and cohesive marketing plan is equally as important as the original business plan. In fact, most competent advisors propose that the marketing plan should precede the business plan, because there is no need to devise a business plan unless you have satisfied yourself as to the extent of the market, how to access it and how to grow your share.

Marketing plans differ among companies but should contain certain basic characteristics and meet certain basic requirements. There is no template for a successful marketing plan, although it is advisable to remember Rudyard Kipling's 'six honest servingmen': Who, What, Where, When, Why and How.

Any plan must be entirely tailored to you and to your business or idea. It must be integrated into the total planning effort of the person or company. It should be appropriate to what you want to do and the risks you are willing to take. It must achieve certain commercial objectives. Finally, it must be feasible, in that it is capable of being achieved.

While this may seem a tall order for any individual, especially for a budding entrepreneur, it is helpful to note that, although our entrepreneurs in this book all started with a plan, that plan changed and evolved so much over time that it bore no resemblance to the original document.

Look at one of our entrepreneurs, Pat McDonagh: his original plan involved opening a pool hall in Ballinasloe, Co Galway. Planning issues arose (the external environment had changed) and hence his plan had to be altered and modified. The point is that nothing is written in stone, you are not married to any particular plan or strategy. All successful entrepreneurs are willing to adapt, or even scrap a plan, if circumstances dictate. But, first, you need the plan.

As previously discussed, an ability to evaluate the potential of the market is essential. Our entrepreneurs all began their projects with an evaluation of the market, weighing up the odds of success. A well-defined marketing plan will not guarantee you success in your particular endeavour but it will help you in making the decision on whether you should go with your instinct. It will help you approach the project in a structured fashion and it will ensure that you are in touch with your potential market. In short, it will considerably increase the odds of success.

It requires no particular abilities. You need no special accounting, sales or administration skills. You need no particular level of education. All you will require is that you spend a little time objectively analysing the marketplace in a structured fashion.

It is essential to evaluate your position, the market's position and the position of your customer. It is not a science. Marketing as an academic discipline has been grossly overrated by many of our third level institutions for many years. Many so-called academics and gurus hold exalted positions, yet they would not survive seconds in the commercial market-place.

Why? Because theorists rarely succeed in practice.

If you look at our entrepreneurs, you will see some of the most competent marketers in this country, or any other country in the world. Much of their ability has been acquired from what Louis Copeland terms 'the school of hard knocks'; in other words, experience is the key ingredient in fine-tuning a marketing and strategic focus. Our interview subjects are good, because they have tried and failed. They are good, because they operate in the real world. Most importantly, they are good, because they took the time to ask the right questions and act on the results.

Marketing is not an art and is certainly not part of the selling process, rather I believe it to be the process of identifying and understanding a customer's needs and requirements and delivering satisfaction to those customers and delivering profits to the business. This is not an art. It is a process, one that can be learnt by anybody.

19: HEALTHY RELATIONSHIP WITH MONEY

Money is one of the vehicles for living well, but it is not the point of living or working, nor the end in itself. Our interview subjects did not set out on their particular road in business just for the money. Yes, it was a major consideration, but not the primary driver of these people. Money is required for living – after that, it appears to become of secondary importance and is used as a tool for keeping score rather than anything else. Our interview subjects are all successful and established, yet it is interesting to note that none of them place much emphasis on money or wealth other than to acknowledge that it is essential for living.

Our entrepreneurs all realise that what you do for a living does not define who you are. Money is simply a medium for keeping score on the health of a business.

You may say that it is easy for them to say that, given that they are established, successful and already wealthy. True, but the point to note is that the accumulation of money for its own sake was not a driving force for our entrepreneurs. They wanted to create something that went beyond money or tangible assets. They wanted to create a business in the organic sense, to establish it, to nurture it and to grow it for its own sake.

20: FIRE IN THE BELLY

All of our interview subjects were, and are, highly motivated. That much seems obvious but, to understand this motivation, we first must understand the individual person, which is way beyond the scope of this book and possibly an impossible task in some of the cases analysed. Nonetheless, it is important to understand the basics of what constitutes motivation.

The motivation that drives our all of our behaviour comes from two sources: internal (intrinsic) and external (extrinsic):

- Intrinsic factors include constructs like needs, desires, motives, and will-power.
- Extrinsic factors include any type of motivational influence from the environment, such as rewards and punishments.

For all our entrepreneurs, the most important motivational factor is the intrinsic one. Entrepreneurs keep going, despite the fact that employees may cause them problems, banks or financial institutions may be difficult, friends may say they are wasting their time, and their family tells them to get a 'real' job.

When the intrinsic drive is absent, so too is any chance of success. In the words of James Bryant Conant, a past president of Harvard University:

The turtle never makes progress until he sticks his neck out.

16
ATTITUDE DEFINES ALTITUDE

The longer I live,
The more I realize the impact of attitude on life.
Attitude, to me, is more important than the past,
Than education,
Than money,
Than circumstances,
Than failures,
Than success,
Than what other people think or say or do.
It is more important than appearance,
Giftedness or skill.
It will make or break an organization,
A school, a home.
The remarkable thing is we have a choice every day
Regarding the attitude we will embrace for that day.
We cannot change our past.
We cannot change the fact that people will act in a certain way.
We cannot change the inevitable.
The only thing we can do is play the string we have.
And that is our attitude.
I am convinced that life is 10 percent what happens to me
And 90 percent how I react to it.
And so it is with you.

Charles Swindell

How important is attitude to success in business? It appears to be more important than you might think. Even if your business offers great products and services at unbeatable prices, the attitude you project will be the factor that makes or breaks it. All the advertising, slogans, buzzwords and promotional campaigns in the world can't mask a business that isn't truly focused on the customer. Likewise, a person cannot mask a poor attitude over the longer term. How many times have you been in a great mood, only to meet someone who looked as if it hurts him or her to smile? This interferes with your own karma and, in turn, influences your own mood. We should all treat people the way they wish to be treated. A bad attitude not only impacts badly on them, it impinges on your personal outlook. A bad attitude can, and will, infect those all around it. Likewise, a positive attitude empowers everyone that it comes in contact with, in every walk of life. Our entrepreneurs all were very definite in their assertion that a positive attitude is the most important attribute a person must have when starting a business or for those looking to succeed in any walk of life.

> *A positive attitude to what you are doing supersedes*
> *everything else – without exception.*
>   Liam Griffin

Senator Feargal Quinn put it very eloquently when he said:

> *Starting a business is a lifestyle choice, as much as anything else. You*
> *need a sense of purpose. If work is no longer a joy, you are likely to fail.*
> *It is imperative you get into a way of life that you will enjoy. Then*
> *your attitude and approach will be right.*

Ultimately, you need to enjoy what you are doing. Your attitude needs to reflect this. There will be bad days, but these are the days when you need a positive attitude most of all.

If this book has unearthed any wisdom from our entrepreneurs, it is that nothing is impossible, given the right attitude. Remember that work is only a chore when you would rather be doing something else.

A study by Harvard University found that, when a suitably qualified person gets a job, 85% of the time it is because of attitude and only 15 % of the time because of other factors.

> *Always bear in mind that your own resolution to succeed*
> *is more important than any other one thing.*
> Abraham Lincoln

> *The greatest discovery of my generation is that human*
> *beings can alter their lives by altering their attitude.*
> William James – Harvard University

> *The future belongs to the common man with uncommon*
> *determination.*
> Baba Amete

ATTITUDE IN THE WORKPLACE

Liam Griffin talks about the attitude of any team having an immense bearing on success, whether it is in business, in the social context or on the field of play. He believes that all groups of people or teams can be roughly divided into three broad groups. The trick as he sees it is to manage the groups and ensure that high achievers are not held back by the others. This is a point that is referred to and developed by all of our entrepreneurs.

Our entrepreneurs identified three groups of people, giving them many different labels, mainly of a complimentary nature. I, on the other hand feel no need to be polite to those who can destroy your personal or professional outlook, so my label for the third group is blunt and direct. The three groups are:

- **Achievers:** These are the people we all wish to be. They are the people that we all gravitate towards at social functions. They exude confidence and energy. They have that indefinable quality called charisma. They have an excellent attitude and approach to life in general and, more specifically, to the team.

They have a positive impact on the dynamic of any team. Such
people are essential to success.

- **Adequate:** Unfortunately, this is where most of us find
  ourselves. The adequate group is exactly as it says on the tin: a
  group of people who fulfil their function but rarely rise above
  mediocrity – foot soldiers. But foot soldiers are essential to
  victory and every team needs its adequate foot soldiers. This
  group interacts with the other groups and are essential to the
  team dynamic.

- **Arseholes:** We can all recognise someone from this group: the
  born cynic, the person who perpetually lives in the valley of
  excuses, the person whose fault or responsibility it never is, the
  person who could be great but for … a million reasons, and of
  course none of them their own fault. This group really does
  exist. We cannot overlook their impact on a team or, more
  correctly, we cannot overlook their negative impact on a team.
  Because, if allowed to prosper, this group will have an
  immense negative impact on the team dynamic and infect the
  adequate group with their negative, cynical deadbeat attitude.
  Stay away from them, ignore them and, whatever you do, do
  not listen to them. They will suck the life force out of you. This
  cannot be understated. Negative people are to be avoided as
  much as is practically possible.

In short, 'dispense with arseholes' should be a personal policy decision
for yourself. Write it down; make it a creed that you live by. Cut them
out of your life now, your life will be greatly enhanced by this act. It is
said that you are the average of the five or six people you are
surrounded by. Can you afford to have your attitude and abilities
compromised by the cynical perpetual underachiever?

Effective business managers waste no time in cutting such people
from a team. Why should you be any different? Life is too short to
waste on losers; surround yourself with winners instead. Start by
identifying the achievers and surround yourself with them. Suddenly,
your average will start to soar. Your personal and professional stock
will rise. You will be on your way, simply because you will have
changed your attitude and enhanced your outlook.

Remember the old saying:

It's difficult to soar like an eagle when you are surrounded by turkeys!

Attitude is everything. It can be regarded as the simple formula for success:

$$\textbf{A} \quad \textbf{T} \quad \textbf{T} \quad \textbf{I} \quad \textbf{T} \quad \textbf{U} \quad \textbf{D} \quad \textbf{E} \quad \textbf{=} \quad \textbf{100\%}$$

1   20   20   9   20   21   4   5   =   100%

ACHIEVING A WINNING DYNAMIC

Managing any business or team is down to how you manage the interaction of the three groups.

The aim, obviously, is to minimise the impact of the Arseholes on the Adequates and Achievers. Successful interaction of the Adequates and Achievers, with an emphasis on ensuring that the Achievers group is as large as possible, is the goal of successful people managers.

All of our entrepreneurs have exhibited an ability to identify where their people fit into the Three A's profile. They have all displayed:

- An ability to show a commitment to foster the recruitment and development of the Achievers.
- An ability to identify, develop and manage the Adequates.
- Crucially, they display absolutely no sufferance of the Arseholes. Once identified, these guys are surplus to requirements. Thus the team dynamic is always strong and exudes energy.

This acquired ability is not unique to our successful subjects. It is not unique to the Irish environment nor is it a product of our time.

In the 1980s, British Airways embarked on a comprehensive Human Resources programme called 'Putting People First' (PPF). The programme studied all of BA's personnel and analysed their suitability for the business, according to the strengths and weaknesses of each employee. This then gave the company an accurate picture of the strength of the entire BA team and how closely aligned the team was to its specific requirements. The results were interesting to say the least.

	Politicians	Winners
ATTITUDE		
	Dead-beats	Cynics

ENERGY

The upshot of this hugely expensive and time-consuming study was that the most desirable individuals are those who fill the upper right-hand quadrant. Winners are more desirable than any other combination of attributes. People who displayed an approach to business and to life in general that was high in energy, high in attitude were the type of people identified by PPF as those who could, and would, contribute most to whatever environment that they found themselves in. Qualifications and skills were only of a secondary importance.

This study was undertaken in a global organisation in the 1980s. It is interesting to note that the results of a scientific study, quantified and empirically-proven, mirror the thought processes and attitude of our chosen entrepreneurs. It seems clear to me that those that wish to succeed in their careers either as an entrepreneur, in an executive capacity or in any walk of life should take personal stock of their personal attitude as it applies to the above diagram (see the next chapter for more).

DOES FORTUNE FAVOUR THE BRAVE?

Analyse the letters below. What do you see? Can you make a sentence from it? Say the sentence once quickly to yourself. Do you say something positive or negative?

OPPORTUNITYISNOWHERE

The reality is that you can read this in two different ways, both of them are correct. But do both ways indicate someone with the same mindset?

The cynic may say that they read 'OPPORTUNITY IS NO WHERE', while a person with a positive attitude might read 'OPPORTUNITY IS NOW HERE'. The interpretation of what you see is dependent on where you position yourself and how you perceive yourself.

Are you positive, energetic and dynamic? Are you easily motivated? Your outlook is NOT preordained. We are masters of our own destiny, but we must believe in ourselves. Pat McDonagh had his plans for a pool hall thrown into turmoil when he was refused planning permission. He refused to be defeated and continued to investigate the potential opportunities. The would-be pool hall became a fast-food restaurant. The fast-food restaurant has become a fast-food empire. If he had opened a pool hall, would Supermac's now exist? Possibly not. We will never know.

But we can see that, as far as Pat McDonagh was concerned, 'opportunity was definitely here' and he was going to seize the chance with both hands. No question and no hesitation, external forces or obstacles were simply there to be overcome. The lack of planning permission simply required a redefinition of his strategy, not a retreat from his goal.

We must believe that having absolute faith in our success is central to our achieving that success. In Rhonda Byrne's excellent book, *The Secret*, this philosophy comes to the fore. As I understand it, at its most basic, *The Secret* refers to the law of attraction in action. You attract everything that comes into your life. Everything without exception. Whatever is going on in your mind, you attract to you. Thoughts become things. If you think it, it will happen. You send signals out into the universe and the universe responds in kind. If you think positive thoughts and have absolute and unwavering faith in a positive outcome, it will happen. This is a powerful book that makes a very powerful argument for positive thinking. I highly recommend that you read it.

In my interview with Michael Herbert, he mentions the central philosophy behind *The Secret*. He acknowledges that he has been living his life according to this philosophy for many years. More importantly, he has the absolute conviction that this philosophy works. Time and time again throughout this book, I was impressed by the positive mindset and attitudes of all of our entrepreneurs. They simply do not contemplate the idea that they cannot achieve their goals. Failure is not ever factored into any of their plans. Certainly, failure is recognised as being possible but it is never important enough to influence the overall goal or plan. They are completely focussed on success. They epitomise the law of attraction in action.

The most startling single thing I uncovered during all of my research and interviews with our business personalities was their diversity: diversity in their personalities, their standards of education, their personal backgrounds and in their interests and opinions. Other than the fact that they were successful in business, they apparently had little in common.

Eventually I got around to examining the evidence I uncovered from the point of view of their personality or more specifically their personal approach to business and all of a sudden I began to see what to me were common traits amongst them.

The critical ingredient is getting off your butt and doing something. It's as simple as that. A lot of people have ideas, but there are few who decide to do something about them now. Not tomorrow. Not next week. But today.

> *The true entrepreneur is a doer, not a dreamer* –
> Nolan Bushnell, entrepreneur and founder of Atari

It all seems to boil down to one word. It covers everything else. Its importance cannot be underestimated. It seems amazing to me that success in business or in life can be attributed to one word, even if there exists much explanation behind that word. The word is: Attitude.

Write it down. Study it. Put it in your bedroom wall. Embrace it, because there is no getting away from it and there is no substitute for it. Every single one of our successful entrepreneurs displayed a positive energetic attitude and crucially identified attitude as being the single most important attribute any person can have.

Michael Herbert best described himself when he said:

I'm positive by nature, I don't like dwelling on the negative.

This attitude and statement could be attributed to any or all of our entrepreneurs. I feel it is their secret to the success of our entrepreneurs as their positive attitude is infectious and empowering.

It is the definitive key common denominator among all of our subjects. It is also the definitive yardstick by which our business successes evaluate potential employees. As Anne Heraty puts it:

It's your attitude all the way that determines your success.

Our entrepreneurs all appear to possess two primary belief systems that drive their behaviour:

- They believe they are 100% accountable for what happens in their business. When things go wrong, they take responsibility and immediately set about to address the situation.

- They also give 100% of the credit to others who deliver, because they know that they cannot be successful without the help of others.

In the main, they exhibited some of the same characteristics in their approach to life, not just in their approach to commerce. These characteristics define their attitude and provide the framework for their success.

At Pragmatica, our people are recognised as being the amongst best human resource professionals in their field. When we are working on an assignment on behalf of a client, we always follow one major dictum:

Hire for attitude – and train for skill.

In other words, all factors being equal, we always start by evaluating candidates on the basis of attitude. A person who exhibits the right positive can do attitude has immense potential: they can be trained in specific processes or skills.

Anne Heraty, CEO of CPL, one of Ireland's leading recruitment firms, summarised the importance of this approach when she said:

> *In today's environment, you need to be IT-literate and have certain*
> *capability around certain skills. But once that's a given, it's your attitude*

all the way that determines your success. Hire for attitude every time,
and train for skill. Every time.

As one of the most successful training and development organisations in
our field, we can state confidently that you cannot properly train or
develop an unwilling candidate or one with a poor attitude. They do not
wish to change or develop and will resist the process all the way. This
philosophy is borne out again by Anne Heraty when she said:

It's your attitude all the way that determines your success.

The point I am trying to make is that no matter who you are or what
you do, your life both personal and professional will be enhanced
greatly by developing a positive 'can do' attitude. Our entrepreneurs all
possess this attitude, all of their staff are hired on this basis and their
friends and social circle all seem to display the same qualities. This is no
coincidence.

Our entrepreneurs are extremely successful because they have made
themselves successful. The first thing they have done is to develop their
attitude and then they have ensured that they have surrounded
themselves with lots of positive attitude. There is no secret formula; it all
boils down to a positive attitude.

Remember that there are three types of people:

- Those who make things happen.
- Those who let things happen.
- Those who say "What happened?".

Which category do you fit into? It really does not matter. What matters
is what category you want to fit into. You can change category quite
easily if you have the will to change. It all boils down to how you
approach life. It boils down to attitude.

Attitude really does define altitude!

17
TAKING PERSONAL STOCK

A common trait amongst our successful business people is the ability to evaluate the reality of their current situation objectively. Like all of life's little secrets, it seems obvious when we look back at it, it just didn't seem as blatantly obvious at the time.

In short, the first rule for anyone entering a commercial environment is to face the current reality of your present situation – confront the brutal facts.

Sometimes, it is helpful to take an aerial view of your entire life by evaluating all of its constituent parts. We often get sidetracked on certain projects or areas within our lives to the exclusion of all else. When life is busy, or all your energy is focused on a special project, it's all too easy to find yourself 'off balance', not paying enough attention to important areas of your life. While you need to have drive and focus if you're going to get things done, taking this too far can lead to frustration and intense stress.

THE LIFE EVALUATION WHEEL

The Life Evaluation Wheel is a very useful tool to get a handle on life's balance. It helps you consider each area of your life in turn and assess what may be off-balance – and thus it helps you identify areas that need more attention.

The Life Wheel is powerful because it gives you a vivid visual representation of the way your life is currently, compared with the way you would ideally like it to be. It is called the 'Life Wheel' because each area of your life is mapped on a circle, like the spoke of a wheel. This makes it easy to use and easy to read.

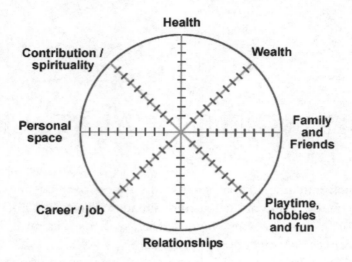

Using the Life Wheel is simple. All you need to do is work from the inside or hub outward and score each of the spokes from one to 10. You then draw a circular line, joining each point and examine the resulting shape.

For a balanced life, the first aim is to have a reasonably circular shape, one that has no major peaks or troughs. If you have a major spike, for example, then the wheel is telling you that you may have to examine the time or energies that you are putting into this area of your life, as it appears that it may be out of balance.

Second, the aim is to develop a strategy within your life to extend the circle outward towards a consistent 10 figure for all of the spokes. This indicates that you are achieving both a balance in your life and are growing as an individual in a balanced fashion.

Remember that you can include or exclude any spokes that you see fit, as no two people have the same ingredients in their lives. I have just covered the rudimentary areas that would appear to be representative of most people. Your wheel should be reflective of your life at any given time and should be unique to you. It should be used as an indicator for you to see whether perhaps you need to put some time and effort into taking stock of your current situation.

All of our interview subjects regularly take stock of their current situation. Louis Copeland is always aware of how much stock his shops carry at any given time. He is a highly competent retailer. He is in charge of his inventory. Equally, he regularly takes stock of where he is both professionally and personally. I like to refer to this type of stocktaking as 'facing the current reality'.

All of our entrepreneurs take stock of their current reality on a regular basis. The busier you are, the more important it is. I venture to suggest that nobody can be successful or achieve their goals unless they first face the current reality. You always need a base from which to embark on a journey – you need a starting point.

When taking the first steps to face your current reality, the results are irrelevant. What matters is that you are taking action. What is relevant is to take stock of your actual situation, objectively and honestly. There is no recognised development programme or development guru in the world that does not begin the development process by an evaluation of the current situation. Pat McDonagh's current situation was that he was refused planning permission for a pool hall. He had to confront the brutal facts and revise his plans. It certainly worked for him. Supermac's has its genesis in his willingness to confront the current reality and to react accordingly. His ability to take action in the face of negative external influences was crucial to the evolution of his business. He redefined his objectives but did not retreat from his goals.

Once an objective and honest analysis has been undertaken, you can act on the results. Once again, it is irrelevant at this time what those facts are, good or bad. What is important is that now you have an inventory of the important issues facing you at this present time. Now you can start to take action.

All of our successful entrepreneurs have displayed clearly an ability to evaluate the position they are in at any given time. This is an ability, not a gift. It is not something our entrepreneurs were born with. It is an ability that can be developed over time. Granted it is not easy, but equally it is not hard, all it takes is application. That is what SWOT analysis is all about.

SWOT ANALYSIS

A useful method for facing the current reality, the SWOT analysis is a basic building block of all business programmes. It is taught on even the most basic programmes. It is taught for a reason. This reason is because it is an immensely powerful tool.

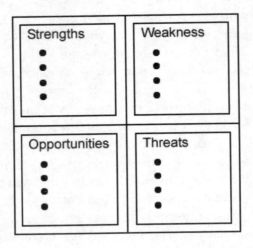

It is effective and simple. It can be applied to all situations and will unearth the current reality, if properly executed. In due course, it will become second nature and should become a key competitive advantage of yours.

Let's get the difficult stuff out of the way right now. You will probably display a much larger list in the two right-hand quadrants. This is not necessarily a bad thing. After all, you are only beginning the process of positioning yourself. Indeed, it is probably true to say that, if you do not have a comprehensive list of negative issues to address it is highly unlikely you have had an objective and honest evaluation, in other words you have failed to face the current reality. In order to take effective remedial action to face the negative situation that has arisen, you must face reality and use this as your starting point.

GAP ANALYSIS

Another useful personal tool for self-evaluation or to face the current reality clearly is to undertake gap analysis. A simple yet effective tool, gap analysis consists of identifying the present state (facing the current reality), identifying where you wish to be (your target) and deciding what you need to do to get there.

Gap analysis alone, however, is not adequate for all problem situations, as goals may evolve and emerge during the course of problem-solving. 'What we wish to happen' can be a highly variable target. It has the advantage of being ideal for focussing the mind on where you wish to be and empowers you to develop a strategy to achieve your goals.

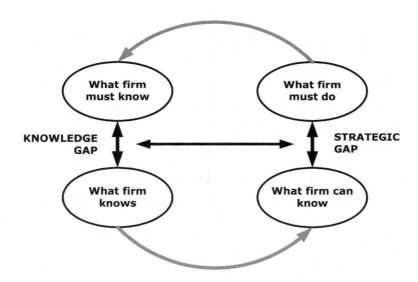

Whatever method you use is really irrelevant. These are just two suggestions that we use regularly. There are many others or you can make up your own. What matters is that the exercise is clear, honest and objective and that it gives you the true picture of where you are at any given time.

Remember one key point: facing reality does not mean we have to accept it.

Reality is always changing. Equally, we can always change reality, all we need is the right attitude. If you have the right attitude, then the right approach eventually manifests itself. All of our entrepreneurs decided to do something, so that they would get to be somewhere. How it was going to happen was of secondary importance.

The destination was the goal but how the journey would be accomplished was of little significance. But without exception, the journey was successfully undertaken.

In facing the current reality, there should only ever be one rule: Do not accept something that you can change!

Never accept something as a given. Anything can be changed. All of our entrepreneurs would have failed at the first hurdle, if they simply accepted something without a challenge. If you believe in something, do not take 'No' for an answer.

THE IMPORTANCE OF SELF-BELIEF

Remember Henry Ford's words:

There are two kinds of people: Those who think they can, and those who think they can't, and they're both right!

In other words, you must believe. If you do not believe in yourself, how can you expect others to have belief in you?

Look at each of our entrepreneurs in this book. Do they lack self - belief? Most certainly, they do not. They do not live in a false world. They have faced the current realities of their situations. They have confronted the brutal facts. Most importantly, they have a positive attitude and they believed they could do it. They believed in themselves, their abilities and then they had a go.

This importance of belief is most evocatively encapsulated in the words of six times *Tour de France* winner and cancer victim, Lance Armstrong, in his wonderful and compelling life story *Its Not About the Bike: My Journey Back to Life:*

But I knew this much: I believed in belief, for its own shining sake. To believe in the face of utter hopelessness, every article of evidence to the contrary, to ignore apparent catastrophe – what other choice was there?

On the entrepreneurial front, Padraig Ó Céidigh has had a number of successful yet varied careers, as a teacher, an accountant, a solicitor, and yet he decided he was going to buy and develop an airline. What prompted him to think he could run and grow an airline so successfully? Having the entrepreneurial idea is one thing but to make a success of a business in one of the world's most brutally competitive sectors with huge barriers to entry is another. To make a success of a business when many of the competitors around the world were going bankrupt required an unwavering faith in his own ability and in the viability of the proposition. In short, he believed in himself. He will tell you himself that, in the early stages of his involvement with the business, he was probably the only one that believed. But there you are, he did it and did it extremely successfully. Aer Arann is now a vital cog in the transport infrastructure of this country. It is profitable and expanding in an industry that is contracting and under immense pressure from external forces. Such is the power of self-belief.

Your progress in life or business tends to consistently follow your expectations. This is a generally accepted and proven fact. It is a self-fulfilling prophecy, and it applies to any field or sector, whether it is personal or professional. If you expect to do poorly, you will be less motivated and less interested; you'll commit less time and energy and thus won't perform as well. Thus you will do poorly, which only serves to reinforce your limiting belief.

Our entrepreneurs implicitly understand that their confidence and the confidence of their team is an organic thing, it grows and multiplies from humble beginnings.

Remember the words of Vince Lombardi, one of American football's most successful ever coaches:

Confidence is contagious.

REACTING TO THE CALL TO ACTION

I have noticed that all of our entrepreneurs have displayed what I term 'a reaction to a call to action'. This means that all of these successful people did not procrastinate when it came to taking action. Once they felt or heard a 'call to action', they immediately got the ball rolling, whether it was simply making the first telephone call, developing a marketing plan or whatever.

The point is that none of them sit on ideas and wait. It is not in their character to hang around waiting. They start the ball rolling with immediate effect. Therefore, the impetus or energy of an idea is never lost. They always seem to enjoy a head start on their competitors, simply because they are first to answer the call to action. Granted, some of the calls to action never amounted to anything – but such is life, not everything works out according to plan all the time.

The point is that our entrepreneurs always took action and did not put the concept or idea on the shelf for another time. That is for dreamers. That is the crucial difference: entrepreneurs do, dreamers dream. Entrepreneurs are dreamers too, but they take action.

UNWAVERING COMMITMENT

It is highly likely that, when one makes an inventory of the difficulties facing the budding entrepreneur, one could say that the odds against success are too great. This highlights another key attribute of all of our successful subjects. They all displayed an unwavering belief and commitment to achieving their goals or to driving their businesses forward. Nobody or no thing was let interfere with the achievement of their goals. Anne Heraty put it succinctly when she said:

> I think that one of the things when you're starting a business is that you've got to understand the completeness of the commitment.

This commitment certainly involves much hard work but it goes much deeper than that. They are willing to sacrifice what they perceive to be of lesser importance in the pursuit of their goals. It is this ability to display an unwavering commitment and to focus exclusively on the task at hand that marks them out as different from the ordinary. This is what makes them special: in a way, it defines them.

It brings us neatly back to our key attribute of attitude. They all displayed an attitude of achievement, no matter what. Obstacles were there simply to be overcome. Challenges were there to be overcome. Limitations could be overcome. Competitors must be overcome. In short, our subjects all show the attributes of a successful fighter, in every positive sense of the word. They will not be swayed, they relish a challenge but, most crucially, they display an unwavering commitment to the achievement of their goals to the exclusion of all else.

It is all down to mindset. The good news is you can develop yours!

DEVELOPING A POSITIVE MINDSET

Developing a positive mindset takes work. There is no fast track or easy method. But, once you've achieved the right outlook, you are empowered to choose who you are and what you want to be. A positive mindset can be very powerful and very influential in your life. It is something that can be acquired by anyone by simply making a decision to think and act differently.

To help change what you believe and how you think, you should investigate the ideas of the people you admire. All of our entrepreneurs closely monitor what is happening in their industry, in industry in general and in the economy as a whole. They consistently make references to other business people and certain characteristics, traits or actions that they have taken that they admire. They take the time to study people, especially successful people in a variety of fields. They meet them, imitate them and try to improve on their positive characteristics.

The Japanese call it *'kaizen'*, a process of planned and continuous improvement. This is the central philosophy behind the Toyota operating practices and is well-explained in *The Toyota Way* by Jonathan Keller. At its most basic, the idea is relatively simple: there is no radical process, no revolution, no epiphany or 'Eureka!' moments, just a slow and inexorable focus on getting it better next time, every time. It's worth learning more about.

Our entrepreneurs all exhibited this approach to business. It was often subconscious, rarely as defined or planned as *kaizen* but it amounts to the same thing. Our entrepreneurs are all extremely curious and interested in learning how to be better, how to do things better, how to gain an advantage in every walk of life.

They expose themselves to positive and motivational people, to ideas and environments. Although these alone will not transform you into a person with a positive mindset, the experience may suggest a plan that can help you become more positive and optimistic. At worst the experiences will place you in the right mindset to proceed. And this is half the battle.

Unless you expose yourself to the ideas of positive and successful people and avoid the exponents of habitual negative thoughts and lifestyle, you will not develop into a person with a positive mindset. I noted the way our entrepreneurs spoke. It was always positive and upbeat. They might have been having a bad time personally or professionally, but I sure did not know it. They all exuded positive vibes and confidence. Their positivity in itself told a story about them. It was a good story!

If you wish to commit to changing your personal headspace, change the way you talk by not complaining. Simply put, if you can't say anything positive, don't say anything at all. Positive affirmations are a popular tool to acquire a positive mindset.

Some people advise writing positive things on paper 20 times daily. There are a few key points to remember when documenting positives:

- State the positive.
- Include your name.
  In the present tense.
  Be very specific.
- Add in the word "now".

For example, here is a positive written statement:

> *Pearce Flannery is now writing the best book ever to be written on the subject of Irish business personalities.*

As you focus on acquiring a positive mindset, it is important to document your goals and objectives daily. Start a journal with nothing but goals, accomplished objectives and aspirations. As you implement your plans, document all your successes in your journal. Gradually, you will learn to view the person in the mirror with renewed respect and admiration.

Developing a positive mindset is one of the most powerful and most rewarding life strategies there is. Positive thinking and a powerful attitude toward life is an essential key in life success and having a healthy mind and body. Positive mindset is your key to success in life and in business. At a personal level, it will transform your life, your health and renew your passion for life. Professionally, you can use the power of a positive mindset to create success and reach your financial goals. Positive people can recognize opportunities and realize their potential. In short, they know exactly what it is to be lucky and how to take advantage of lucky breaks when they arise. Negative people fail to recognize opportunity when it is presented to them. Positive people expect to succeed and negative people expect to fail. Whether you believe you can or cannot achieve something you are right. So why not believe that you can.

It is up to you to make the choice. There is no secret, no formula and it is definitely not something you are born with. It is a skill that can, and should, be learnt. Ultimately, you can shape your life. All it takes is a little work. Choosing to have a positive mindset will allow you to attract amazing opportunities and successes in your life. Our successful entrepreneurs all developed a positive mindset and none of them were born with it.

There is nothing to stop you developing a successful mindset – except you!

18

DEVELOPING INTERPERSONAL SKILLS

WHAT MATTERS MOST IS HOW YOU VIEW YOURSELF

How do you view yourself? It appears that a positive personal perception is a vital ingredient of entrepreneurial success. Our interview subjects are confident in themselves and comfortable with their inner selves. By this, I mean that they are confident in their personal abilities. Equally, they are able to acknowledge their commercial limitations and to ensure that they put in place structures to compensate for any limiting factors that became apparent. This confidence is reflected in their outlook and personalities: they exude a confidence that overtly demonstrates that they are comfortable with who they are. In short, they like themselves, in a positive and constructive way.

Do you like yourself? How do you perceive yourself and your abilities? Do you believe you have the potential and tenacity to succeed? Personal perception is inextricably linked with many of the characteristics outlined in **Chapter 15** and is dependent on many of the factors outlined being in place.

However, there was another trait or characteristic that is evident in all of our entrepreneurs. It is intangible and indefinable, although it is an intrinsic part of what these people are and is more important than a characteristic – it is an integral part of their personalities. It is self-esteem.

It is difficult to define, as each of us as an individual is different and has many differing and defining characteristics. Just as no two people are alike, no two people have the same self-perception. A person's self-perception is as unique as their fingerprint or their DNA.

Maslow's Five Needs

In 1943, Abraham Maslow one of the founding fathers of humanist approaches to management, developed a triangular matrix that set out five fundamental human needs and their hierarchical nature. They are quoted and taught so widely now that many people perceive this model as the definitive set of needs and do not look any further. A key aspect of the model is the hierarchical nature of the needs. The lower the needs in the hierarchy, the more fundamental they are and the more a person will tend to abandon the higher needs in order to pay attention to sufficiently meeting the lower needs. For example, when we are ill, we care little for what others think about us: all we want is to get better.

Maslow's five needs are:

- **Physiological needs:** These are to do with the maintenance of the human body. If we are unwell, then little else matters until we recover. Pain and discomfort can range from mild to excruciating, and will have a proportionate effect on our rate of abandoning higher needs.

- **Safety needs:** These are about putting a roof over our heads and keeping us from harm.

- **Belonging needs**: These introduce our tribal nature. If we are helpful and kind to others, they will want us as friends.

- **Esteem needs**: These are for a higher position within a group. If people respect us, we have greater power. Esteem basically is about self-esteem, which is feeling good about ourselves. We can get such esteem in two ways: internally, we can judge ourselves and find ourselves worthy by our own defined standards; most people, however, start with the outside, seeking social approval and esteem from other people, judging themselves by what others think of them.

- **Self-actualisation needs**: These are to 'become what we are capable of becoming', which would be our greatest achievement. We would probably refer to it as fulfilling our potential.

In essence, this model demonstrates that once we achieve our most basic of needs such as health and welfare, food and shelter, then another stream of needs, wants and desires automatically kicks in. This follows upward to the point where all of our basic needs are fulfilled and we are faced with the need for self-esteem.

As our other more basic needs are fulfilled, the need for self-esteem becomes our most motivating force.

Our perception of how others see us is an integral part of how we see ourselves. Hence, we can see that, for normally adjusted individuals in a developed society, their self-perception is part of what and who they are. They care about how they are perceived and ensure they have a positive self-perception.

Self-esteem in the sense I am outlining is not big-headedness or arrogance, although most big-headed and arrogant people would have an inflated sense of self. High self-esteem has long been considered a virtue in other countries, yet in Ireland it is often regarded as some form of arrogance. This is a fault of the Irish psyche, as we should all hold ourselves in high esteem – if we don't, how can we expect others to think highly of us? Nowadays, we see a paradigm shift in Irish society, and not before time. The trait is encouraged in students, celebrated among executives, and expected in celebrities.

Our entrepreneurs never let their levels of self-esteem drop. This is often subconscious, but they are adept at maintaining their personal self-image. This is the way it should be. We should take a leaf out of their books and do likewise. By raising self-esteem, we will realise a wide variety of benefits in our professional and personal lives. Those with high self-esteem are more effective in their communication ability, and more likely to establish richer, more rewarding relationships.

People with greater self-confidence possess a more positive expectation for the future. They feel good about their ability to accomplish a result and so they are more pro-active, are in more focused action, and have less of a tendency to sabotage themselves along the way as those lacking self-esteem typically do.

Those believing in their abilities are less driven to prove themselves as worthy and so they are less prone to burn-out. They relax more and tend to have fun more often and are less stressed, since they have less to prove. Those with a higher self-image are also more likely to appreciate their accomplishments.

In their personal lives, people with high esteem tend to be more at peace. There is some evidence that couples possessing high self-esteem typically fight less with each other and tend to do better in sustaining long-term relationships. They tend to get along better with others. As we have outlined throughout this book, business is an environment run by people. Thus a person's ability to relate to, and get on with, people is crucial to their chances of success in this arena.

These comments seem to mirror the personality traits of our entrepreneurs. Is this chance? Decide for yourself.

SELF-CONFIDENCE: A NECESSARY INGREDIENT

Self-confidence is a necessary ingredient for success. Self-confidence sells. It sells the person, the concept, product or service. It's something you can sense about a person upon entering a room. It's evident through body language and speech. All of our interview subjects had a quiet, self-assured confidence that was evident from the beginning. This was most certainly not arrogance or cockiness, rather it was a confidence in their own ability to cope with situations, a confidence built up over many years' experience of themselves. Our interview subjects understood themselves, knew their own capabilities and were happy in their own skins.

They unconsciously radiated this attribute, because they evidently did not have to even think about it. It is now second nature to them.

They have learnt how to be confident, because they know what it is like to make mistakes and have realised that mistakes can be dealt with and overcome. Likewise, they are equally adept with coping with success and do not let it overpower them.

It's not just what they say, but how they say it. It's important to realise that you can create self-confidence. You don't have to be born with it. Everyone is capable of learning how to be incredibly self-confident. It's like most other things: it can be learnt.

THE POWER OF CHARISMA

Charisma is a word is derived from the religious Latin term 'charisms', meaning 'gifts of the Holy Spirit'. Our entrepreneurs are all charismatic, high-energy individuals. This is in no small way a result of their positive 'can do' attitude. It is infectious and I am convinced that developing charisma is a skill just like typing, communicating or driving. If the attitude and energy is there, the rest can easily be put in place. Contrary to some schools of thought that assert that charisma can be learned through a 1-2-3-step process, I believe that it is an ability that increases as the skill is embraced and developed. Surveys consistently show that charismatic people make more money and generally are more successful than their counterparts. Invariably, charismatic people have an edge, even when they are not as technically proficient as their counterparts. Likewise, people who are deemed charismatic are more fun to be around, connect with more people and develop relationships that lead to greater income potential, in addition to invitations to forums where opportunities present themselves. This is fact.

Is it a coincidence that charismatic people are more successful and that all of our entrepreneurs are charismatic? I think not. Such a personality trait has been an integral part of their success. Because they are responsible for fostering the development of this facet of their character, we can confidently state that they are responsible for their success. Luck had little or nothing to do with it.

PERSUASIVE TECHNIQUES: MOTIVATING PEOPLE

Interestingly, none of our successful entrepreneurs considered motivating their people to be a particularly difficult task. Their people seemed to be relatively easily motivated and the business leaders clearly do not view the process of motivation as an onerous chore. This most likely relates to the personality and character of our interview subjects. There are possibly a number of reasons for this.

First, I believe it is primarily down to the fact that our entrepreneurs surround themselves with people of a similar outlook to themselves. They are very choosy in recruiting for key positions and, therefore, usually recruit people with the right attitude and commitment to the organisation. This dynamic percolates right through the organisation. Our entrepreneurs rightly realise that the right people do not need much in the line of motivation, since they are self-motivated individuals. However, our subjects recognise that it is essential that they create an environment that does not foster the onset or development of de-motivation.

Second, because the culture of the organisation is fused with people in key roles with the right attitude there exists a form of energy in the organisation. This energy enables the entire team to self-motivate. The old saying 'Nothing breeds success like success' comes into play here. People who realise that they are important to any organisation get a sense of belonging, one of ownership. They then place a value on the organisation to which they are part. They belong to it and it to them.

Padraig Ó Céidigh points to a member of staff who joined Aer Arann as an aircraft technician after many years at Aer Lingus. He told Ó Céidigh that, at Aer Lingus he felt that he was just fixing planes, but at Aer Arann he was building an airline. He had a sense of belonging, a sense of ownership.

Third, our subjects all display an innate ability to lead people. They lead by example, but equally they lead through discipline. Not in the autocratic sense, and certainly not in the sense of being dictators, but equally they do not give themselves to consensus if the direction being taken does not meet their expectations. They are able to provide clear and unambiguous direction: they lead and others follow. If not, then the team and the team dynamic may need to be re-appraised. However, it is equally important to note that each of our entrepreneurs listens to suggestions from colleagues and employees. They listen, evaluate the quality of the message and then act. It is true that they often overlook or overrule good ideas or suggestions but the key point is that they make a decision and then take action.

Liam Griffin supports this stance most eloquently when he says:

> *By being in charge, you can get results, and somebody has to take responsibility. And I just hope that we are entering a new era where people say, "We're listening to you. We hear you. But this is now how we're going to do it. It's fair, we've taken your ideas on board, but we're going to do it this way. That's leadership".*

Finally, each of our entrepreneurs highlight the importance of building a good team around them and attribute their success to this particular attribute. Rarely do they hire the wrong person for a particular role. On the rare occasions that they do, they are not afraid to take action and to replace the weak link in the team. They have developed an ability to see the capabilities within people. More importantly, they have developed the ability to get the best out of people. Another way of putting it is that their people are happy to commit to them and give them their best efforts. They display a loyalty and commitment to their people and, in return, they engender loyalty and commitment from their colleagues.

It is important to note that the art of persuasion is a developed ability and not some inherent gift that was somehow bestowed on them at birth. The ability to be persuasive can be learnt and anybody serious about personal development in their lives or in their business should work toward developing competence in this area.

We all recognise certain people who would be regarded as persuasive, good communicators, good at getting people to agree with them. This ability is an essential attribute for success. It is a valuable tool for every person and having this ability will make everybody's walk through life a little more pleasant.

Once again, there is some good news: we can all improve our persuasive techniques; we can all become better at dealing with people. It simply requires practice and a concerted ability to identify and empathise with your subject. Put simply, you must always try to see the other person's point of view; you do not necessarily have to agree with it but you must acknowledge their point of view and understand their position. In doing this, it is essential to let your subject see clearly that you are interested in them and their opinions. Documented below are some areas that you can work on to enhance your persuasive techniques and to develop your interpersonal abilities. This is not science, it all relates to treating your subjects with a certain level of courtesy and respect and, crucially, that your subject sees that you are treating them in this manner.

DEVELOPING YOUR INTERPERSONAL SKILLS

Understand, Empathise and Listen to People

In short, all of our interview subjects are 'people people'. They have developed the ability to listen and understand. This is not as easy as it seems. People send messages in a variety of ways. I found this ability to understand people so important to the entrepreneurs' overall ability, I decided to research it a little further. It makes for an interesting study.

Obviously, people can articulate their feelings in verbal or written form. But, surprisingly, of the three broad communication groups, words only account for 7% of our communication.

Words can be:

- Visual (I see what you mean).
- Auditory (I hear what you are saying).
- Kinaesthetic (I get a sense of what you are saying.)

Be under no illusions – all of our participants have demonstrated that listening is a skill, not a gift. It can be learnt. My subsequent research has uncovered four main levels of listening:

- Non-listening.
- Marginal listening.
- Evaluate listening.
- Active listening.

We often overlook the fact that words are spoken at a rate of 90 to 200 per minute, but they can be heard at a rate of 400 to 500 per minute. If the speaker does not match the listener's rate in some way, the listener has a tendency to drift or become distracted.

The experts recommend that we listen with questions in our mind.

All of our survey participants conveyed an ability to display honesty, empathy and respect for people. This is always reciprocated. In the words of Feargal Quinn on his approach to political life:

I try to look for the customer behind every piece of legislation.

Likewise, successful people managers look for the person behind every employee or colleague. We buy from people, we hire people and we empathise with people.

Louis Copeland calls it 'hugging the hugger'. His frontline personnel are there to metaphorically hug the customer, to make them feel valued, important and special. He crucially recognises that, from time to time, someone needs to hug the hugger.

Tone accounts for 38% of your communication. Tone can be referred to as the image your voice creates. The pitch, the volume, the tempo or the inflection, all conspire to overpower the actual message contained in the spoken word. The tone tempers the perception of what someone is saying and hence becomes the reality of the statement. For example, sarcasm often relies on tone for effect.

Develop the ability to listen for tone in people's messages; your ability to understand people will become much sharper.

Body language accounts for 55% of communications. So, in addition to hearing what someone says, we need to *see* what people say.

Body language analysis is a science in itself. There are many outstanding books on the subject. The core philosophy is that, if you get into a place where you are actively trying to understand and empathise with people, your body language will become conducive to connecting with the person. You will subconsciously mirror their actions and body language.

It is interesting to note that our society spends the first 12 years or so of our lives teaching us the skills to read and write properly and yet words account for less than 7% of the overall communications package. Few people even know that there is so much more to effective communications.

Study it; get good at it and you will be amongst the select few. You will be empowered. You will give yourself an advantage in life as well as in business. Your life chances will increase immeasurably.

Seeing the Other Person's Point of View

I have noticed that, in managing people, our entrepreneurs try to understand the constraints their people operate under. This enables them to see both sides of the argument and to make objective decisions. Crucially, these decisions are usually compatible with the wishes of the team and, therefore, the harmony or team dynamic remains intact. In other words, our successful entrepreneurs try to understand all of the working areas of their respective business, by spending a considerable amount of time on the shop/factory/office floor. This is often referred to as 'management by walking around' (MBWA). It keeps them in touch with the present reality and ensures that they do not lose touch with their people. All of our entrepreneurs realise to some degree that the business action is not all behind their own desks. It is happening for real out on the shop/factory floor. They hold random meetings in other people's offices or on the floor. They get out there. They do not hide behind barriers or closed doors.

All of our entrepreneurs, without exception, have stated that they love what they do and do not look on it as work; rather, it is a labour of love. They love their job and this is evident. It radiates out of them, it is infectious and our subjects are infectious in their approach or enthusiasm. Their enthusiasm motivates and empowers everyone around them. It's amazing how, if you hate your job, it seems like everyone else does, too. If you are very stressed out, it seems like everyone else is, too. Enthusiasm is contagious. If you're enthusiastic about your job, it's much easier for others to be, too. Also, if you're doing a good job of taking care of yourself and your own job, you'll have much clearer perspective on how others are doing in theirs.

A good place to start learning about motivation is to start by understanding your own motivations. The key to motivating people is to understand what motivates them. No two people are alike, so we need to examine our approach to those around us. So what motivates you? Consider, for example, time with family, recognition, a job well done, service, learning, etc. How is your job configured to support your own motivations? What can you do to motivate yourself better? People can be all fired up about their work and be working very hard; however, if the results of their work don't contribute to the goals of the organisation, then the organization is not any better off. Therefore, it's critical that managers and supervisors know what they want from their employees.

Different things motivate different people. Our entrepreneurs all acknowledge this from early on. They realise the importance of the team around them and the importance of each member within that team. Their situations and circumstances change, so their motivations or desires will change. Our entrepreneurs all understand and work at ensuring that they keep abreast of what is happening in the lives of their teams. It is an ongoing process to sustain an environment where employees can motivate themselves. Our interview subjects continually look at sustaining employee motivation as an ongoing process.

In Feargal Quinn's wonderful book, *Crowning the Customer*, he discusses how he puts the customer first. The customer comes first, before anything and everything in every way. This philosophy defines the operating ethos of the whole business. For example, his shop managers did not have an office: all meetings were held on the shop floor, enabling managers to be within the reach of the customer and staff at all times and in touch with the customer at all times. This was just one example of the huge effort he put into developing a customer-focussed culture in his organisation. I strongly recommend this book: it is a must for anyone serious about developing a customer-oriented business.

All of our entrepreneurs have displayed an ability to understand people and to empathise with them as individuals, as well as members of a team. This enables them to understand what they are dealing with and to manage their human resources effectively. Once again, this is not a gift, nor is it a characteristic we are born with. It is an acquired ability, one that has its genesis in the ability to listen to people: to really listen to people and not just pay them lip service. All good managers have developed this ability, as have all good sales professionals.

As a generalisation, it seems fair to say that one person cannot actually motivate another, although they can have an affect on facilitating the motivational process. Employees and teams in general have to motivate themselves. Our entrepreneurs realise that you can't motivate people anymore than you can personally empower them. Employees have to motivate and empower themselves, but you can help with the process.

Our entrepreneurs all work towards setting up an environment where their people can best motivate and empower themselves. They all seem to start with ensuring that they lead by example, they show that that themselves are motivated and enthusiastic about what they are doing. They realise that they cannot expect their people to get enthusiastic about something, if they themselves are not passionate and committed to the same cause. Enthusiasm is contagious. If they enthusiastic about their job, it's much easier for others to be, too. Also, if they are committed to doing a good job, the team will have a much clearer perspective on how they are doing in theirs.

Different things motivate different people. You may be greatly motivated by earning time away from your job to spend more time my family. You might be motivated much more by recognition of a job well done. People are different. They are not motivated by the same things. Successful business leaders all work toward understanding what motivates each of their key employees.

Our business personalities commence the motivational process or dynamic before they ever hire anybody. They are conscious that a person's characteristics and attitude are the most essential attributes required in the make-up of a good team player. They ensure that their people all have the required attributes and undertake rigorous scrutiny during the selection process for key personnel. If the material is right in the first place, then all factors being equal, the people should be able to motivate themselves given the right environment.

Our entrepreneurs are facilitators. They facilitate their people by providing the correct environment within which they must operate. They then lead by example. After that, it is very much down to the attitude, approach and energy of the particular employee. If the employee is having difficulty in self-motivation at this stage, they are unlikely to be with the organisation for very long.

Empathise with Their Needs

Likewise, all of our entrepreneurs display an empathy with the customer. You must understand your customer or you cannot meet their needs. The customer is at the centre of everything a business does. It may seem obvious but yet, at Pragmatica, many of our clients have lost their customer focus. This is usually the root cause of whatever problem they have asked us to address.

Therefore, let me say it loud and clear, lest there be any confusion: the only reason to be in business is to get, and keep, customers!

One should never forget this message. To forget this is to die, commercially speaking.

If you do not respect your customers, if you do not speak to your customers, if you do not understand your customers, you will fail. This is an absolute. You will never change my mind on this point and you will find no exceptions to this rule. To succeed in your chosen field, develop the ability to understand people. This is achieved by learning to really listen to them and to empathise with them. Never forget that all the stakeholders in your business are real people with real feelings, dreams and aspirations. Remember this point, treat all your contacts with respect and courtesy, it will always be reciprocated. It will enhance your success and abilities in whatever field you chose to operate in. The success of our entrepreneurs in such a diverse range of industries is the proof of this theory.

SUMMARY

Someone once said that the journey is the destination. As regards writing this book that is certainly the case. This project seems unfinished, incomplete in itself and yet the experience of meeting, interviewing and deciphering the thoughts of such a talented group of people, to me, has been the defining experience of this project.

The analysis in this book just scratches the surface of the secret of entrepreneurial success. It is a subject that merits intensive study and would make a wonderful PhD thesis. However, I believe that even the most in-depth comprehensive studies undertaken on this subject anywhere cannot escape the following simple observations as being essential to entrepreneurial success:

- A positive 'can do' attitude is essential to success.
- A positive self image and self-confidence is essential.
- Always hire the best and build a good team.
- Respect for people, employees, customers – even competitors.
- An ability to work hard.
- Fortitude in overcoming setbacks.

Finally, one vital and significant point to note from all of these investigations is important to highlight. None of the attributes required for success in the commercial environment are gifts or some form of endowed talent. The capacity required to succeed can be developed and learnt. This is not some formal academic study, it is about personal positioning and the development of the right attitude. It can be done; it is being done every day. But it does require determination and a lot of hard work. I say hard work because I have deliberately left the one most important defining characteristic of our entrepreneurs till last: a willingness to work hard!

Good luck!
Pearce Flannery
September 2008

ABOUT THE SPONSORS

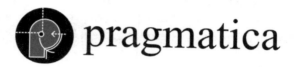 pragmatica

The Pragmatica Group was established initially as a firm dedicated to improving operational capabilities within the hugely competitive automotive sector. Pragmatica Automotive developed a reputation for innovation and achievement and rapidly evolved into the market leader in its sector. Since then, many businesses from all walks of life have used Pragmatica's services, culminating in the establishment of a separate business trading as Pragmatica Commercial. These two businesses are part of the Pragmatica Group.

The Group's mission statement *'Transforming Business Through Empowerment'* reflects a philosophy of improving operations using the resources at hand. Massive improvements can be made through the efficient use of existing personnel and processes, without costly investment in infrastructure and resources.

The Pragmatica team is supported by an extensive range of retained contractors and strategic alliance partners to ensure that the right people with specific skill sets are used for each individual project.

Broadly speaking, the business splits into two divisions:

1) **Management & Marketing:** This award-winning division provides operational analysis and consultative support, with an emphasis on ensuring that the client develops the required capabilities and expertise to continue to manage its own process of continuous improvement.

2) **Human Resources:** Incorporating its highly acclaimed Training & Development Department and its specialist Executive Search & Selection operation providing recruitment services to its growing client base.

Pragmatica is based in Galway, with offices in Leixlip, County Kildare and Northampton in the United Kingdom. Its international partner, Autopolis, has a global network of offices, including London, Paris, Sydney, Istanbul, Detroit and Hong Kong.

Further information can be accessed from the following websites: www.pragmatica.ie / www.autopolis.com.

Contact details for Pearce Flannery or any of the team at Pragmatica are available from: info@pragmatica.ie.

INDEX

OAK TREE PRESS

is Ireland's leading business book publisher.

It develops and delivers
information, advice and resources
to entrepreneurs and managers –
and those who educate and support them.

Its print, software and web materials
are in use in Ireland, the UK, Finland,
Greece, Norway and Slovenia.

OAK TREE PRESS
19 Rutland Street
Cork, Ireland
T: + 353 21 4313855
F: + 353 21 4313496
E: info@oaktreepress.com
W: www.oaktreepress.com